THE ESSENTIAL
Thomas Paine

PAINE

THE ESSENTIAL
Thomas Paine

Thomas Paine

EDITED BY
John Dos Passos

Dover Publications, Inc., Mineola, New York

Bibliographical Note

This Dover edition, first published in 2008, is an unabridged repub-
lication of *The Living Thoughts of Tom Paine,* originally published by
Longmans, Green and Co., New York, in 1940. The woodcut portrait
of Thomas Paine was made by Professor Hans A. Mueller.

Library of Congress Cataloging-in-Publication Data

Paine, Thomas, 1737–1809.
  [Living thoughts of Tom Paine]
  The essential Thomas Paine / Thomas Paine ; edited by John
Dos Passos.
       p. cm.
  Originally published: New York : Longmans, Green, and Co.,
1940.
  ISBN-13: 978-0-486-46600-2
  ISBN-10: 0-486-46600-0
  1. Political science. I. Dos Passos, John, 1896–1970. II. Title.

JC177.A5 2008
320.51092—dc22

                                                           2007043738

Manufactured in the United States of America
Dover Publications, Inc., 31 East 2nd Street, Mineola, N.Y. 11501

THOMAS PAINE

I

O ye that love Mankind! Ye that dare oppose not only the tyranny but the tyrant, stand forth! Every spot in the old world is overrun with oppression. Freedom hath been hunted round the globe. Asia and Africa have long expelled her. Europe regards her like a stranger and England hath given her warning to depart. O receive the fugitive and prepare in time an asylum for mankind.

When Tom Paine wrote out these words in his level, plain readable handwriting, sitting in some smallwindowed lodging or in the back room of a tavern in the booming money-grubbing Quaker-run port of Philadelphia, he told just about the literal truth. He was at work on *Common Sense*, the pamphlet that was to put into plain daily talk of wharves and stores and counting-houses and country alehouses and of bunches of farmers, artisans, merchants standing around church doors under trees after meeting, men's not yet quite formulated thoughts. It was plain that once the thoughts were put into words, the words would have to be put into acts, and that right away.

It was the fall of 1775. Paine had been in America a year and had found there exactly what he had been looking for all his life : freedom, a world that gave him a chance to use his great abilities. Now the hopeful growth of that world was challenged by the army of the Crown, and its defense endangered by the timidities and vacillations of the men of substance and respectability in the colonies, who were afraid of losing what they owned. Paine was no scholar : like many men of parts of the time he had largely gotten his education from conversations in taverns and coffeehouses, and from lectures and newspapers. Writing, for him, was the direct putting down of plain speech.

The struggle between George III, the most astute manipulator of practical politics England had seen for a long time, and the colonies over their rights and franchises, had for a while seemed to run parallel with that king's wrangle with the cities of London and Westminster over electoral corruption that ended with the seating of Wilkes; but gradually it was coming over the people in the colonies that, in this case, the Crown had no intention of giving in, and that what was intended was their complete subjection.

It was not for nothing that George's German mother had raised him in sober habits of industry and had pounded into his head the admonition: George, be a King. Outside of England absolute government was the rule in Europe. On the whole continent, only in the tiny citystate of Geneva could a man not of the highest rank go about his business and say his own say without being in daily dread of the police. George believed it his duty and privilege to give his subjects the benefit of a similar orderly rule. The house of Orange had succeeded in bullying and bribing the Dutch out of their liberties and reducing the States General to a wordy formality. The same thing could be done in England. George had a civil list of a million and a half pounds. He was willing to spend every shilling of it to promote the royal power, and every hour of his day in manipulating the delicate machinery of rotten boroughs, places, careers, titles through which he controlled his government. He wore himself out with the patient work of corruption. The corollary to "George, be a King" was "Every man has his price."

At home the method of "gold pills" was proving remarkably effective. In spite of the fact that the King's

Men had been forced to allow Wilkes and his fellow-members to be seated in the new parliament that met in November 1774, the opposition was only able to muster seventy-three votes on the first division. "I am not sorry," George wrote, "that the line of conduct seems now chalked out, which the enclosed dispatches [describing the seditious performances of the colonials] thoroughly justify. The New England governments are in a state of rebellion. Blows must decide whether they are to be subject to this country or independent."

In America the blows had begun. The Crown had started the war with the occupation of Boston. The Americans had answered with the blockade. By the fall of seventy-five, there was no British authority left in the thirteen colonies. The country was policed by the towns and counties and the committees of correspondence that had their centre in the Continental Congress in Philadelphia. George Washington had accepted the command of the Continental Army and was busy at his headquarters in Cambridge trying to get together shoes and muskets, and to drill troops of desultory militiamen into an organized force.

Instead of "resistance" people were beginning, with considerable dismay, to say "war." To Paine it must have seemed as if the Crown had followed him across the sea to shut him up again in the narrow slum that eighteenth-century England was for the plain man, hemmed in on every side by the walled privileges of rank and fortune.

2

Up to the time that Paine arrived in Philadelphia at the age of thirty-seven, with a bundle of essays in his baggage, his life had been one failure after another. He was born in 1737 in the old Saxon and Danish town of Thetford in Norfolkshire when Robert Walpole, that hard-headed fox-hunter, a Norfolk man himself,

was running the country. Tom Paine was brought up
in a section of English society almost as far removed
from the half-German court that centred around the
fat irritable German king and his mistresses and his
frankspoken queen, and the wit and the speculations of
courtly writers, and the fox-hunting and wine-guzzling
of the gentry, as America itself.

He was the son of Joseph Pain, a master corsetmaker, a freeman of the town, and a Quaker. His
mother was the daughter of an attorney or notary, and
possibly thought of herself as a notch above her husband in the social scale. Their marriage is on record
at the local established church and the biographers have
dug up a story that she and a sister of hers took little
Tom to be confirmed by the bishop. Anyway the
moral climate in which Paine was brought up was that
of the dissenting tradespeople and artisans of the English towns, who since the time of the Lollards had been
individualists in religion and tended to republicanism
in politics. As the only dissenters in Thetford were
the Quakers, Paine's youth must have been moulded by
the peculiar restraints of Quaker meeting. He was not
allowed to study Latin at school because the Quakers
found the classical authors indecent and bloodthirsty.
When at an early age he ran away to sea at Kings Lynn
and signed up for service on the privateer *Terrible*
with a skipper who had adopted the sonorous name of
Captain Death, his father promptly went after him and
brought him home again. Still the fact that his father's
shop, where Paine was put to work as soon as he was
through grammar school, was a corsetmaker's, must
have given it a trace of connection with the powdered
London world of modish strut and foppery and hard
drinking and free thought, if only through fashion
plates, but it must have been a very faint trace. Long
after he was out on his own he wrote :

Though I reverence their philanthropy, I can't help smiling at the conceit that if the taste of a Quaker had been consulted at the creation, what a silent and drabcolored creation it would have been. Not a flower would have blossomed its gaieties nor a bird been permitted to sing.

There was little of flowers or birds singing around the stout oak boards they cut whalebone on in the stuffy corsetmaker's shop, so before long young Paine ran away again, this time for keeps. He seems to have gone to sea for a while on the privateer *King of Prussia,* and then gone to London where he worked as a journeyman corsetmaker in a shop on Hanover Street, Longacre. In his free time he went to public lectures on scientific subjects at the Royal Academy and read the gazettes. He had all his life Franklin's sort of personal interest in science and practical invention.

He doesn't seem to have held any job very long, because in the following year there is a record of his working as a journeyman at Dover. Later he set himself up at Sandwich as a master staymaker, and married. His business didn't do well, or maybe he was too impatient to let it get started. He sold out and moved to Margate where his wife died, possibly in childbirth. He began pulling wires to get an appointment in the Excise. With his father's help he finished the necessary course of study and was sent as a gauger to Alford in Kent. Within a year he'd been fired for laxity in carrying out his inspections.

He set to work to get reinstated, meanwhile picking up a living as a journeyman corsetmaker. He must have been keeping up his education because in 1766 he was usher at Mr. Noble's academy in Goodman's Fields and taught English grammar and syntax. Then he taught school in Kensington until he managed to get another appointment in the Excise. Some of the biographers have circulated a story that during this period

he preached at nonconformist churches and at the then
so popular out-of-door revival meetings, but it seems
a little unlikely, as he never spoke in public in later life.
It's possible that he tried to get ordained in the Church
of England, the natural haven at the time for men of
scholarly or literary tastes. Ignorance of Latin probably blocked him there.

In the winter of 1768 he was appointed exciseman
to Lewes in Sussex, where he went to lodge in an ancient half-timbered house, that had been an inn in the
time of Elizabeth, with a Quaker named Samuel Ollive
who kept there a tobacco shop and grocery. It was
next door to the West Gate dissenters' meetinghouse.
In Lewes, Paine soon got the reputation of being a
good talker and man of nerve, and was known as
the Commodore. When he wasn't going from liquor
dealer's store to liquor dealer's store with his measur-
ing stick and inkbottle and notebook, he was sitting
talking with a group of cronies at the White Hart
Tavern where gathered young men interested in po-
etry and singing and reform politics. Thomas Rickman, nicknamed Clio by the crowd because he composed songs, first knew Paine there and wrote of him
in his fragmentary recollections :

In this place he lived several years in habits of intimacy
with a very respectable, sensible, convivial set of acquaintance, who were entertained with his witty sallies and informed by his more serious conversations. In politics he
was at this time a Whig, and notorious for that quality
which has been defined perseverance in a good cause and
obstinacy in a bad one. He was tenacious of his opinions,
which were bold, acute and independent, and which he
maintained with ardor, elegance and argument. At this
period in Lewes, the White Hart evening club was the re-
sort of a social and intelligent circle who out of fun, seeing
that disputes often ran very warm and high, frequently had
what they called the "Headstrong Book." This was no
other than an old Greek Homer which was sent, the morn-

ing after a debate vehemently maintained, to the most obstinate haranguer in the Club : this book had the following title, as implying that Mr. Paine the best deserved and most frequently obtained it : "The Headstrong Book, or Original Book of Obstinacy, written by — of Lewes, in Sussex, and revised and corrected by Thomas Paine."

At the news of the death of Wolfe in the taking of Quebec, Paine wrote a patriotic ballad to Rickman's music, that became very popular :

In a mouldering cave where the wretched retreat,
Britannia sat wasted with care ;
She mourned for her Wolfe and exclaimed against fate
And gave herself up to dispair.

He is said to have been paid three guineas by a Whig candidate for an election song, and certainly he read humorous verses to the Club over their ale. The impression you get is that he was very much the lion of that particular circle. So much so that when agitation among the excisemen for higher wages and better working conditions came to a boil in 1772 he was asked to draw up a memorial stating their case to be presented to parliament. Paine, who probably didn't enjoy poking his stick into distillers' casks and snooping around back alleys after smugglers much more than he had enjoyed sewing whalebone into ladies' corsets, jumped at the opportunity. He wrote out a soberly phrased appeal to the reason and humanity of the members of parliament, which is his first piece of argumentative writing, and went posting up to London with it on funds subscribed by his fellow gaugers.

Two years before, old Ollive had died and, a few months after, Paine had married his daughter Elizabeth and moved in as the Quaker's successor in business. So now as well as handling the excise he was operating a snuffmill and selling the very tobacco that he stamped. There is a mystery about his marriage to Elizabeth

Ollive. For some reason, which Paine would never tell, they did not live together as man and wife. Possibly he looked upon the marriage as a mere business partnership. According to Rickman he always spoke affectionately of his wife, and Conway discovered that years after their separation she went on using an intaglio of his head as her seal on business papers. If we knew more about it, I think we would find here one of the keys to the man behind the brilliant barroom arguments, the fervent pamphleteering, the reckless dedication to the truth, as well as to his inordinate frank vanity, his occasional hard drinking, the trouble he often had in getting on with people, and the lonely old bachelor's life he led to the end. Although he had many women friends, it seems unlikely that he ever slept with a woman from this time on. Certainly he had no permanent domestic relationships. From now on he was a public character. The entire man was projected into the political exhorter. Of his inner self we know very little.

When Paine came back from London after having singularly failed to interest parliament in the woes of so unpopular a class of men as the excisemen, the precarious but perhaps satisfactory way of life he had managed to build up at Lewes collapsed all at once. His fate was that of many an agitator for better hours and wages since. He was fired from the excise and this time for good. Almost the same day this notice was put up at Lewes :

To be sold by auction, on Thursday the 14th of April, and following day, all the household furniture, stock in trade and other effects of Thomas Pain, grocer and tobacconist, near the West Gate in Lewes : Also a horse tobacco snuff mill, with all the utensils for cutting tobacco and grinding off snuff; and two unopened crates of cream colored stoneware.

One thing Paine got out of his winter's lobbying in London was an introduction in the coffeehouses to men of the great world of letters and politics. He got to know Oliver Goldsmith and Franklin. When his life at Lewes collapsed, he sold out the store, signed articles of separation from his wife, renouncing any rights to what property she may have had left, and went back to London, and the talk in the taverns, and the newspapers, and the American question. England now held for him only bitter memories of frustration and defeat ; it was inevitable that like so many before, like so many after him, he should set out for the west.

In the fall of 1774 he took passage for Philadelphia carrying a letter from the great Dr. Franklin suggesting that Richard Bache, his son-in-law, "put him in the way of obtaining employment as a clerk, or as assistant tutor in a school, or assistant surveyor, of all of which I think him very capable, so that he may procure a subsistence at least, until he can make acquaintance and obtain a knowledge of the country."

By March of the following year Paine was writing back from Philadelphia to Dr. Franklin :

Your countenancing me has obtained me many friends and much reputation, for which please accept my sincere thanks. I have been applied to by several gentlemen to instruct their sons on very advantageous terms to myself, and a printer and bookseller here, a man of reputation and property, Robert Aiken, has lately attempted a magazine, but having little or no turn that way himself, he has applied to me for assistance. He had not above six hundred subscribers when I first assisted him. We have now upwards of fifteen hundred and daily increasing.

He was editing the *Pennsylvania Magazine* or American Museum, indeed writing most of it himself, including the descriptions of mechanical inventions. People with a taste for letters and humanitarian thought were seeking him out, and finding a slender man with very bright eyes and a sharp nose, dressed in Quakerish drab and snuffcolor and wearing a bob-tailed wig, full of ardor against the restraints of the crumbling world of feudal privilege and arbitrary royal rule, ready to argue at the drop of a hat about the problems of the day or to discuss a steam engine or a new model lathe or a better shape for a wax candle. In Philadelphia he grew mentally and morally as fast as a seedling transplanted out of a cramped seedbed into rich well-watered soil.

Franklin wrote back, "Be assured my dear friend, that instead of repenting that I was your introducer in America, I value myself on the share I had in procuring for it the acquisition of so useful and valuable a citizen." The *Pennsylvania Magazine* had become a focus of the reforming spirit of America. There appeared in it articles against African slavery, duelling, the subjection of women, cruelty to animals ; in favor of liberal divorce laws and arbitration of international disputes, and a few hints on the possible need of separating completely from the British Crown. Written in the common speech of the day, in a hardheaded argumentative tone, the magazine was something new in journalism. Through it flowed all the practical humanity, the townsman's canniness and the faith in man's unaided reason that had been accumulating underground among the shopkeepers and craftsmen of the English-speaking world during the century and a half since the failure of their first great political outburst in the Commonwealth. In the British Isles the growth of this class had been checked. It had become encysted in the complicated apparatus of British society. In America the great empty continent gave scope to its enormous stored-up energy.

3

Old Franklin seems to have seen from the first that Paine had the qualities that were needed to put the feelings of the Americans into words. Paine wrote later telling of the inception of *Common Sense* :

Dr. Franklin proposed giving me such materials as were in his hands towards completing a history of the present transactions and seemed desirous of having the first volume out the next spring. I had then formed the outlines of Common Sense and finished nearly the first part ; and, as I supposed the doctor's design in getting out a history was to open the new year with a new system, I expected to surprize him with a production on that subject much earlier than he thought of ; and without informing him of what I was doing, got it ready for the press as fast as I conveniently could, and sent him the first pamphlet that was printed off.

Common Sense hit the problem dead in the eye. People thought for a while that Franklin or John Adams had written it. Even a man so slow to make up his mind as Washington (who had declared, on being questioned about independence by the Reverend Jonathan Boucher when their boats met in the middle of the Potomac river one day in May of that same year while Washington was being ferried across on his way to the Continental Congress, "If you ever hear of my joining in any such measures, you have my leave to set me down for everything wicked") wrote on January 31, 1776, to Joseph Read (referring to the burning of open towns by the British fleet), "A few more of such flaming arguments as were exhibited at Falmouth and at Norfolk, added to the sound doctrine and unanswerable reasoning contained in the pamphlet Common Sense, will not leave numbers at a loss to decide upon the propriety of separation."

Hundreds of thousands of copies of *Common Sense* were sold.   With the reckless disregard for his personal interests that was characteristic of him all his life, Paine told the printer to turn the profits over to the treasury of Congress and set to work to elaborate his arguments in the *Forester* letters.   For the first time since the days of the Commonwealth the republican doctrines in politics that were inseparable from the individualist trend of the protestant reformation in religion were put down in popular form.   This time they were linked to the practical notions about representative government that had been the basis of the agitation in England against the rule of the royal moneybags and the rotten borough system.   Almost overnight the theory upon which the United States government was to be laid out was in every man's mouth.

At that moment Paine's temper and train of thought exactly matched popular needs.   The moment was not to last very long.   For the rest of his life he was to go on, with complete disregard of the consequences to himself, fervently explaining his doctrines and checking them with complete candor to meet transforming events.   He had the best nose of any man who ever lived for the political happenings of the moment.   He never let himself drift with the tide.   His journalistic pieces and letters urging this or that cause form one of the most acute critical descriptions we have of the great changes in the life of western Europe he lived through. The extraordinary courage and steadfastness with which he held to his basic conceptions, in favor and out of favor, makes his career of the greatest interest to generations like our own who are living through a similar period of changing institutions.

The word and the deed were always very close with Paine.   Right away he acted on his belief "that those who expect to reap the blessings of freedom must like men undergo the fatigues of supporting it," and enlisted in Roberdeau's "Flying Camp," a kind of irregular shock brigade enlisted for the summer of 1776. When the Flying Camp broke up he joined another rejected Quaker, that sadfaced Rhode Islander who was later to have the thankless job of quartermaster general of the Continental Army, Nathanael Greene, as volunteer aide de camp at Fort Lee. After the loss of New York, Paine retreated with the ragged forces to Newark. There he wrote, so tradition has it, on a drumhead by a campfire, the first of the *Crisis* papers that did so much to keep up the spirits of Washington's disorganized and beaten army. "These are the times that try men's souls" was the watchword of the sentries the frosty morning after Christmas when Washington, to win his only clearcut victory in the painful years up to Yorktown, crossed the Delaware and surprised the Hessians in Trenton ; and then brilliantly escaped being bottled up in the town by Lord Howe's superior forces by breaking camp in the middle of the night, leaving fires burning and pickets singing out one to another ; and, after a desperate march over soggy halffrozen logging roads, where tired men, marching halfasleep, stumbled and sprawled over felled trees, appeared in the British rear at Princeton and so alarmed his lordship that he hastily marched back to winter quarters in the direction of the Hudson.

That ended the campaign for the winter. Paine got back to Philadelphia in time to be complimented by being sent as a commissioner to treat with the Indians at Easton. In April 1777 he was made secretary to Congress's Committee for Foreign Affairs, a post which he held until January 1779 when he resigned after the row about the circumstances of the French loan to the colonies. Paine was afraid that Congress was being shaken down by a group of financial highjackers in Paris, led by the playwright Beaumarchais, possibly with the connivance of the American agent Deane, and

published the story in the papers. Congress was forced
to disown him at the request of M. Gérard, the French
minister, who was keeping up a diplomatic fiction that
there was no French aid at all. Publication of documents in the matter gives the impression that Paine was
right ; but he found himself unpopular in many powerful quarters. During a good deal of Paine's incum-
bency Congress was in flight and Paine was escorting
his chest of highly inflammable documents over the
rutted wagontracks of Pennsylvania and New Jersey
just one jump ahead of the redcoats. Excerpts from
a letter of Paine's to Franklin give the flavor of life in
the lines after the fall of Philadelphia :

The 11th of September last I was preparing dispatches for
you when the report of cannon at Brandywine interrupted
my proceeding. The event of that day you have doubtless
been informed of, which, excepting the enemy keeping the
ground, may be deemed a drawn battle. General Washington collected his army at Chester, and the enemy's not
moving towards him next day must be attributed to the
disability they sustained and the burden of their wounded.
On the 16th of the same month the two armies were drawn
up in order of battle near White Horse on the Lancaster
road, when a most violent and incessant storm of rain prevented an action. Our army sustained a heavy loss in their
ammunition, the cartouche boxes, especially as they were
not of the most seasoned leather, being no proof against the
almost incredible fury of the weather, which obliged General Washington to draw his army up into the country until
those injuries could be repaired, and a new supply of ammunition procured. The enemy in the mean time kept on
the west side of Schuylkill. On Friday the 19th about one
in the morning the first alarm of their crossing was given,
and the confusion, as you may suppose, was very great. It
was a beautiful still moonlight morning and the streets as
full of men, women and children as on a market day. On
the evening before I was fully persuaded that unless something was done the city would be lost ; and under that anx-

iety I went to Colonel Bayard, Speaker of the House of Assembly, and represented, as I very particularly knew it, the situation we were in, and the probability of saving the city if proper efforts were made for that purpose. . .

The retreat was as extraordinary. Nobody hurried themselves. Every one marched his own pace. The enemy kept a civil distance behind, sending every now and then a shot after us, and receiving the same from us. That part of the army which I was with collected and formed on the hill on the side of the road near White Marsh church ; the enemy came within three quarters of a mile and halted. . . I breakfasted next morning at General Washington's quarters, who was at the same loss with every other to account for the accidents of the day. I remember his expressing his surprise, by saying, that at the time he supposed everything secure, and was about giving orders for the army to proceed down to Philadelphia ; that he most unexpectedly saw a part (I think of the artillery) hastily retreating. This partial retreat was, I believe, misunderstood, and soon followed by others. The fog was frequently very thick, the troops young and unused to breaking and rallying, and our men rendered suspicious to each other, many of them being in red. A new army once disordered is difficult to manage, the attempt is dangerous. . .

General Washington keeps his station at the Valley Forge. I was there when the army first began to build huts ; they appeared to me like a family of beavers : every one busy ; some carrying logs, others mud, and the rest fastening them together. The whole was raised in a few days, and is a curious collection of buildings in the true rustic order. . .

For my own part, I thought it very hard to have the country set on fire about my ears almost the moment I got into it ; and among other pleasures I feel in having uniformly done my duty, I feel that of not having discredited your friendship and patronage.

In the spring of 1778 the British pulled out of Philadelphia leaving the city more Tory than before, in spite of the fact that three thousand of the inhabitants followed the British fleet to New York, and Congress and its supporters straggled back into a sullen town. The evacuation was due more to the surrender of Burgoyne after the battle of Saratoga in the preceding winter than to the immediate military situation. The clash of powers in Europe was bringing about an open break between England and France. In February Lord North himself had made conciliatory proposals to the colonies in parliament, and the government theory now was that everything could be settled by sending commissioners to arrange terms. The king submitted to this humiliation, but the one thing he balked at was the one thing that might have made conciliation effective, a ministry under Chatham, the elder Pitt. Anyway events were moving too fast. On May 4th Franklin's Treaty of Alliance and Commerce with France was ratified by Congress in Philadelphia. Already a French fleet was hovering off the mouth of the Delaware. Vergennes had decided that the time had come to give the old enemy England a knockout blow. The rebellion of the colonies merged into a world war ranging from the north Atlantic to India.

After resigning from his official post Paine, who always lived from hand to mouth, found himself out of funds. The French minister seems to have made some effort to employ him as a propagandist for the French but Paine was too independent for him. He supported himself working as a clerk for Owen Biddle, keeping the newspapers hot meanwhile with letters on public concerns. In a letter to Henry Laurens about his project for writing a history of the revolutionary war, and asking incidentally for a loan, he wrote :

I find myself so curiously circumstanced that I have both too many friends and too few, the generality of them thinking that from the public part I have so long acted I have no less than a mine to draw from. What they have had from me they have got for nothing, and they consequently suppose I must be able to afford it. I know but one kind of life I am fit for, and that is a thinking one, and of course a writing one — but I have confined myself so much of late, taken so little exercise, and lived so very sparingly, that unless I alter my way of life it will alter me. I think I have a right to ride a horse of my own, but I cannot now even afford to hire one, which is a situation I never was in before, and I begin to know that a sedentary life cannot be supported without jolting exercise.

All through his life Paine was to be in the same quandary. When he had any money, he would subscribe it to some cause or other or give it away when his debts ran up on him he would be forced to make humiliating appeals to friends and public men. He never formed the knack that successful men have of encrusting themselves in official niches. He didn't have the respectable coloration of the country gentleman that protected many of the great libertarians of the time. His function was to observe events with the gazette in his hand from his seat in the coffeehouse or tavern and say his say and let his private life go to hell, and it did.

This time the Pennsylvania Assembly came to his relief by making him its clerk. On the very day of his appointment an act was introduced for the freeing of negro slaves within the Commonwealth.

The spring of 1780 was a bad time for Washington's army. There were desertions and mutinies everywhere. The Continental currency was about worthless. After such stubborn resistance and such hardwon successes it seemed as if the movement for independence were going to collapse from war-weariness and plain lack of money. It was Paine who read one of the gloomiest of the Commander-in-Chief's many gloomy letters to the Pennsylvania Assembly. "I assure you every idea you can form of our distresses will fall short of the reality. There is such a combination of circumstances to exhaust the patience of the soldiery that it begins at length to be worn out, and we see in every line of the army the most serious features of mutiny and sedition." Immediately Paine headed a subscription for the relief of the army with the five hundred dollars of back salary that remained to be paid to him.

All the following year he was interested in the question of raising money and in February 1781 he was appointed to accompany young Colonel Laurens, the son of his friend Henry Laurens, to Paris in a last desperate attempt to get some hard cash out of Vergennes. The mission was thoroughly successful. By the first of June, Paine and Laurens were sailing from Brest on a fast French frigate with 2,500,000 livres in silver and with a shipload of clothing and munitions in convoy. American fortunes had begun the slow climb that culminated in the surrender of Cornwallis at Yorktown the nineteenth of the following October.

On November 30, Paine, broke again, wrote to Washington from his lodgings on Second Street in Philadelphia, where presumably the landlady was beginning to enquire about the rent :

It is seven years, this day, since I arrived in America, and though I consider them as the most honorary time of my life, they have nevertheless been the most inconvenient and even distressing . . . While it was everybody's fate to suffer I cheerfully suffered with them, but tho' the object of the country is now nearly established and her circumstances rising into prosperity, I feel myself left in a very unpleasant situation. Yet I am totally at a loss what to attribute it to ; for wherever I go I find respect and every body I meet treats me with friendship ; all join in censuring the neglect and throwing blame on each other, so that their civility disarms me as much as their conduct distresses me.

Washington answered by arranging with Robert Morris and Livingston for Paine to be paid a salary of eight hundred dollars a year out of the secret funds of the Secretary for Foreign Affairs. At this period Paine and Washington were good friends. In Washington's papers there is a note from Paine inviting him "to spend a part of an evening at my apartments, and eat a few oysters or a crust of bread and cheese" to discuss some public business of a secret nature. Paine was considered the official mouthpiece for Congress on foreign affairs. From the beginning he was backing with every means in his power the idea of a strong central government against the centrifugal tendency of the states. So great was his influence that he was asked to go to Rhode Island to try to get the Rhode Islanders to give up their opposition to the import duties Congress was trying to levy to pay enough of the interest on the foreign indebtedness to keep up the credit of the infant United States in the world money market.

Meanwhile he had managed to buy himself a house and lot at Bordentown, New Jersey, where he settled near his old friend the Colonel Kirkbride he spoke of in his letter to Franklin years before. Probably he was already tinkering there with his model for an iron bridge that was going to share his time about equally with his journalistic writing during the next few years.

In September 1783 the British reluctantly recognized the independence of the United States. Congress was at Princeton, where a mansion, Rocky Hill, had been fitted up for Washington. Conway quotes a Rhode Islander's letter home describing dinner at the General's :

The tables were spread under a marquise or tent taken from the British. The repast was elegant but the General's company crowned the whole. As I had the good fortune to be seated facing the General, I had the pleasure of hearing all his conversation. The President of Congress was seated on his right and the Minister of France on his left. I observed with much pleasure that the General's front was

uncommonly open and pleasant; the contracted pensive
phiz betokening deep thought and much care, which I no-
ticed at Prospect Hill in 1775, is done away and a pleasant
smile and sparkling vivacity of wit and humour succeeds.
On the President observing that in the present situation of
our affairs he believed that Mr. Morris had his hands full,
the General replied at the same instant, he wished he had
his pockets full too. On Mr. Peters observing that the man
who made these cups (for we drank wine out of silver
cups) was turned a Quaker preacher, the General replied
that he wished he had turned a Quaker preacher before he
made the cups. You must also hear the French minister's
remark on the General's humour. "You tink de penitence
would have been good for de cups." Congress has ordered
an Egyptian statue of General Washington, to be erected
at the place where they may establish their permanent resi-
dence. No honors short of those which the deity vindi-
cates to himself can be too great for Gen. Washington.

Paine had been complaining, as he did fairly frequently, that he was being neglected, and the General
must have gotten wind of it, because he wrote him a
graceful letter inviting him to Rocky Hill. In his article on the causes of yellow fever Paine gives an account of an evening very characteristic of the men and
the time :

We had several times been told that the river or creek
that runs near the bottom of Rocky Hill, and over which
there is a mill, might be set on fire, for that was the term
the country people used ; and as General Washington had
a mind to try the experiment, General Lincoln, who was
also there, undertook to make preparation for it against the
next evening, November fifth. This was to be done, as
we were told, by disturbing the mud at the bottom of the
river, and holding something in a blaze, as paper or straw,
a little above the surface of the water.

Colonels Humphreys and Cobb were at that time aides-
de-camp of General Washington, and those two gentlemen and myself got into an argument respecting the cause.

Their opinion was that, on disturbing the bottom of the river, some bituminous matter arose to the surface, which took fire when the light was put to it ; I, on the contrary, supposed that a quantity of inflammable air was let loose, which ascended through the water and took fire above the surface. Each party held to his opinion, and the next evening the experiment was to be made.

A scow had been stationed in the mill dam, and General Washington, General Lincoln and myself, and I believe Colonel Cobb (for Humphreys was sick), and three or four soldiers with poles, were put on board the scow. General Washington placed himself at one end of the scow and I at the other ; each of us had a roll of cartridge paper, which we lighted and held over the water about two or three inches from the surface when the soldiers began disturbing the bottom of the river with the poles.

As General Washington sat at one end of the scow and I at the other, I could see better anything that might happen from his light than I could from my own, over which I was nearly perpendicular. When the mud at the bottom was disturbed by the poles, the air bubbles rose fast, and I saw the fire take from General Washington's light and descend from thence to the surface of the water, in a similar manner as when a lighted candle is held so as to touch the smoke of a candle just blown out, the smoke will take fire and the fire will descend and light up the candle. This was demonstrative evidence that what was called setting the river on fire was setting on fire the inflammable air that arose out of the mud.

Paine lived at Bordentown until the spring of 1787, at work, with the help of an English mechanic named John Hall, on the model for a projected bridge across the Schuylkill, corresponding with members of the Philosophical Society on scientific subjects, and meeting all the chiefs of the young republic in long wrangles over politics in Franklin's library in Philadelphia. Meanwhile his friends tried to induce various state legislatures to make him grants in return for his services. Madison and Jefferson failed to accomplish anything for him in Virginia because the Virginians were riled by his pamphlet opposing their pretensions to ownership of about everything west of the Allegheny mountains. Already his frank republicanism was making enemies among men of property. Still Congress made him a present and the State of New York gave him a farm with a fine mansion on it that had been confiscated from a New Rochelle Tory. He was now in a position to settle down as a country gentleman, to buy up Continental paper and options on western lands and to marry and found a family and to go down in history as one of the Founding Fathers. He did none of these things.

4

In the spring of 1787 Paine found himself in the unusual position, for him, of having money in his pocket to travel with. For a number of years he had been anxious to go back to his old home in England. "My father and mother," he wrote Franklin, "are yet living, whom I am very anxious to see, and have informed them of my coming over." Then there was the matter of the bridge ; the conservative business men of Philadelphia couldn't make up their minds to put up the money for the unheard of experiment of an iron span across the Schuylkill. Perhaps in France he would find someone willing to take a chance. He sailed from Philadelphia on the April packet and went straight to Paris with his wooden model that he'd been showing off in Franklin's back garden. He spent the summer in Paris, in close touch with Jefferson, trying to promote interest in his bridge, but succeeded only in getting a theoretical endorsement from the Academy of Sciences, and went over to England in the fall. There he found that his father had died the year before. He was able to make his mother, who was nearly ninety, comfortable with a weekly allowance in the old house on Heathen-

man Street in Thetford. He stayed with her all fall
correcting proof on a new pamphlet, *Prospects on the
Rubicon*, that urged young Pitt's government to keep
away from a European war long enough to let the
growing forces of reason start to work in France.
Paine was losing no time in jumping into politics.

For once libertarian ideas were fashionable. The
years up to '91 were the honeymoon period of the En-
lightenment in Europe. London and Paris were closer
than they have ever been since. The French reform-
ist nobles, military men and writers, and the freethink-
ing clergy and the humane ladies of the drawingrooms
of the old regime were full of admiration for the British constitution. The British reforming whigs, Charles
James Fox and his friends, who were so American they
wore Washington's buff and blue in Parliament and
at Brooks', spent as much of their spare time as they
could in Paris. Good society clicking red heels in the
Faubourg St. Germain, and the upstart crowds that
poured into the arcades out of the gambling houses
and restaurants of the Palais Royal (soon to be called
Maison Égalité) were equally humanitarian. Enlighten-
ment was spreading through Versailles and the Louvre.
Washington was the hero of the courts and coffeehouses of Europe. Anybody who had any connection
with America was equally a nine days' wonder in London and Paris.

Paine seems to have gone soberly about his business
in England, spending a great deal of time at Walker's
ironworks at Rotherham in Yorkshire, where they were
building a large size model of his bridge, and where,
far into the nineteenth century, visitors were shown
the hammer and anvil he used, and his leather apron,
and old workingmen told them with awe in their voices
about his kindness, and his sharp tongue : the most
honest man that ever lived. He was invited to the
whig country houses and spent a week with Edmund

Burke. Everywhere he found America fashionable, and a vague diffusion of liberal sentiments, and the feeling that Europe was on the verge of great events.

Royall Tyler met him in London about this time and put down a slightly malicious description of him :

He was dressed in a snuffcolored coat, olive velvet vest, drab breeches, coarse hose. His shoebuckles of the size of a half dollar. A bobtailed wig covered that head which worked such mickle woe to courts and kings. If I should attempt to describe it it would be in the same style and principle with which a veteran soldier bepraiseth an old standard : The more tattered, the more glorious. It is probable that this is the same identical wig under the shadow of whose curls he wrote Common Sense, in America many years before. He was a spare man, rather under size, subject to the extreme of low, and highly exhilarating spirits ; often sat reserved in company ; seldom mingled in common chit chat : But when a man of sense and elocution was present, and the company numerous, he delighted in advancing the most unaccountable, and often the most whimsical paradoxes which he defended in his own plausible manner. If encouraged by success or the applause of the company, his countenance was animated with an expression of feature which, on ordinary occasions, one would look for in vain, in a man so celebrated for acuteness of thought ; but if interrupted by an extraneous observation, by the inattention of his auditory, or in an irritable moment, even by the accidental fall of the poker, he would retire into himself, and no persuasion could induce him to proceed on the most favorite topic.

He crossed the channel several times back and forth between London and Paris, mostly on business connected with the bridge. From England he wrote constantly to Jefferson who was American minister in Paris :

My model and myself had many visitors while I was at the works. A few days after I got there, Lord Fitzwilliam, heir to the Marquis of Rockingham, came with Mr.

Burke. The former gave the workmen five guineas and invited me to Wentworth House, where I went and stayed a few days.

This bridge I expect will bring forth something greater, but in the meantime I am like a bird from its nest, and wishing most anxiously to return. Therefore as soon as I can bring anything to bear I shall dispose of the contract and bid adieu. I can very truly say that my mind is not at home.

I am very much rejoiced at the account you give me of the state of affairs in France.

On the whole he couldn't fit into English society; life in America had more in common with the dissenting middleclass England of his upbringing, with Thetford and Lewes, than did the ruling class England his fame now introduced him to, but where he could never feel himself in anything but a tolerated position. The caste system had probably not the iron grip on English life it now has, but even then a tradesman and the son of a tradesman could never really belong to the top layer that held the levers of power. Like most imaginative Americans Paine was happier in Paris than in London. And Paris was now the epicentre of the great upheaval that was to transform Europe and to cut Paine off from England forever.

May 1, 1790, he wrote Washington from London :

Our very good friend the Marquis de la Fayette has entrusted to my care the Key of the Bastile, and a drawing handsomely framed, representing the demolition of that detestable prison, as a present to your Excellency . . . That the principles of America opened the Bastile is not to be doubted, and therefore the key comes to the right place . . . I am returned from France to London about five weeks ago, and am engaged to return to Paris when the Constitution shall be proclaimed, and to carry the American flag in the procession. I have not the least doubt of the final and compleat success of the French Revolution. Little Ebbings and Flowings, for and against, the natural companions of revolutions, sometimes appear ; but the full current of it is, in my opinion, as fixed as the Gulf Stream.

Already a split was appearing in the humanitarian whig movement that for a while after the American peace had seemed to contain the whole future of British institutions. Charles James Fox had written a few days after the fall of the Bastile : "How much the greatest event it is that ever happened in the world ! How much the best !" and had sent his compliments to the Duke of Orléans, whose courtly libertarian faction at that time was the fair counterpart of the group of fashionable wearers of the buff and the blue, friends of the rounder Prince of Wales, who made up Fox's whigs. He added that "all my prepossessions against French connections for this country will be at an end, and indeed most part of my European system of politics will be altered if this revolution has the consequences that I expect." This was quite in line with what Paine had been urging in *Prospects on the Rubicon*. A few days later Edmund Burke was writing to Lord Charlemont : "The spirit it is impossible not to admire ; but the old Parisian ferocity has broken out in a shocking manner. It is true that this may be no more than a sudden explosion ; if so no indication can be taken from it ; but if it be character rather than accident, then that people are not fit for liberty, and must have a strong hand like that of their former masters to coerce them."

As the landslide in France gathered speed and it became obvious that more and more ancient fences would be broken down, Burke, who was a thoroughly humane man, but one of those many emotional Irishmen who have made themselves by their abilities a home in the English system, and in the end have come to love and reverence every machicolated anachronism of that complicated pile with a pious zeal from which the native English are quite free, began to feel that everything he had attained was in danger : the ermine spotted hierarchy, the country houses, the green hedges that kept the mob off the cropped lawns of the great estates, the port wine and the oratory and the intimate chuckle that went around the benches of the Commons after a well delivered classical quotation. He had seen what the mob could do at the time of the Lord George Gordon riots ; the English mob ; now he saw the French mob, twice as bloodthirsty and unkempt, pouring out of the Faubourg St. Antoine. In a growing panic he wrote *Reflections on the Revolution in France.* The occasion for it was a reforming sermon by Dr. Price, who with Burke and Fox, had been a powerful defender of American rights.

Even before the *Reflections* was published in November 1790, radicals and whigs were talking about it. Long after Price and Priestley had their doubts of Burke's progressive opinions and Burke and Fox had broken off their long friendship, Paine, who hated to believe ill of a friend, clung to the idea that if someone argued with him reasonably he would come to see that if the Bastille and the feudal walls that were confining the peoples of Europe were to go down, some of the beautiful green ivy that had overgrown them would have to go too. In the preface to the first edition of *Rights of Man*, which he wrote at breakneck speed to answer Burke's argument, he said in a childishly frank tone of disappointment :

From the part Mr. Burke took in the American revolution, it was natural that I should consider him a friend to mankind ; and as our acquaintance commenced on that ground, it would have been more agreeable to me to have had cause to continue in that opinion than to change it.

At the time Mr. Burke made his violent speech last winter in the English parliament against the French Revolution and the National Assembly, I was in Paris, and had written him but a short time before to inform him how prosperously matters were going on. Soon after this I saw his advertizement of the pamphlet he intended to publish . . . I promised some of the friends of the Revolution in that country, that whenever Mr. Burke's pamphlet came forth I would answer it. This appeared to me the more necessary to be done, when I saw the flagrant misrepresentations which Mr. Burke's pamphlet contains ; and that while it is an outrageous abuse of the French Revolution and the principles of Liberty, it is an imposition on the rest of the world.

The first part of *Rights of Man* came out in March 1791. It was immediately widely read and spread all over England through the great radical societies which had grown up out of the reform movement. It stated the fundamental principles of representative republicanism in the language of markets and docks and counting-houses ; it was circulated so cheaply that even the common people could read it. Members of the British ruling class began to feel the rope round their necks : *les aristocrats à la lanterne*. Burke felt that his ponderous head was already on a pike. Again Paine had caught the tide of opinion on the flow. *Rights of Man* made him the leader of the republicans in France and the radicals in England. At the dinner of the Revolution Society (a society of dissenters that met every year to celebrate the fall of the Stuarts and the coming of toleration with William of Orange) at the London Tavern in November 1791, Paine was the centre of enthusiasm. A song had been specially composed in his honor :

He comes — the great Reformer comes.
Cease, cease your trumpet, cease, cease your drums . . .
The joyful tidings spread around,
Monarchs tremble at the sound :
Freedom, freedom, freedom, freedom ;
Rights of Man and Paine resound.

Paine's toast in answer to the ovation was : The Revolution of the World !

But Paine had none of the qualities of a political leader : he remained the journalist, the pamphleteer, the political commentator. As it wasn't considered safe for him to live at an inn in the face of the growing opposition to his doctrines, he lived with his friend from the old days at Lewes, "Clio" Rickman, who had set himself up as a bookseller in London, and who in his fragmentary "Life" put down years later what he remembered of Paine's habits during that period in London :

Mr. Paine's life in London was a quiet round of philosophical leisure and enjoyment. It was occupied in writing, in a small epistolary correspondence, in walking about with me to visit different friends, occasionally lounging at coffeehouses and public places, or being visited by a select few . . . At this time he read but little, took his nap after dinner, and played with my family at some game in the evening, as chess, dominoes and drafts but never at cards ; in recitations, singing and music, etc. ; or passed it in conversation : the part he took in the latter was always enlightened, full of information, entertainment and anecdote. Occasionally we visited enlightened friends, indulged in domestic jaunts and recreations from home, frequently lounging at the White Bear, Picadilly, with his old friend the Walking Stewart (an eccentric Scotchman who travelled all over Europe and the Near East on foot examining the state of the world), and other clever travellers from France and different parts of Europe and America . . . Mr. Paine in his person was about five feet ten inches high, and rather athletic ; he was broadshouldered and latterly stooped a little. His eye, of which the painter could not convey the exquisite meaning, was full, brilliant and singularly piercing ; it had in it "the muse of fire." In dress and person he was generally very cleanly, and wore his hair cued, with side curls, and powdered, so that he looked altogether like a gentleman of the old French school . . . In

mixt company and among strangers he said little, and was
no public speaker.

Meanwhile every gazette and every mail from France
widened the rift between the radicals, who felt that
the Revolution of the World was at hand, and the conservative whigs.   One of those transformations of opinion, so hard to put into words but so typical of English
history, had taken place.   Under Pitt a new group had
imperceptibly merged with the old whig and tory
gentry to form a new ruling class.   Pitt's ministry represented the booming banking and shipping interests of
the cities even more than it represented the country
gentlemen getting rich off the enclosures which were
driving the workers into the slave pens of machine industry.   With the news that George III was mad, a
thoroughly characteristic revulsion of feeling towards
him had gone through all classes of English society.
Suddenly he became the loved and powerless monarch
so dear to British institutions.   The power was, since
the election of 1784, firmly in the hands of Pitt, who
thoroughly understood the needs of business and industry ; and whose funding system was going to pay
off the national debt, so shipowners and speculators and
Indian millionaires told each other over their port.
    In America the first result of the new constitution
and of the assumption of the confederate debt, by which
the speculators in continental paper became suddenly
a great financial interest under the nurturing care of
Alexander Hamilton, produced in the Federalists a party
of men of substance thoroughly sympathetic to Pitt's
administration.   The Adamses read *Rights of Man* with
almost as much holy indignation as Burke ; and even
Jefferson, rapidly becoming the leader of the republicans in America, was embarrassed by the endorsement
that was placed without his consent on the American
edition by the printer, although he privately admitted

that he considered the book most valuable ammunition against the Federalists who, he feared, were willing to go as far as absolute monarchy to keep government in the hands of the right people.

In England, Pitt, the young reformer, for a while was very quiet about what was happening in France, pleased on the whole to see the collapse of Bourbon power ; but the minute it looked as if the contagion might spread to England, he threw his projects of electoral reform into the wastebasket, and started to organize the police power to protect the grand edifice of carefully balanced privilege and graft that Burke, with tears in his voice, was apostrophizing as the British Constitution. First he seems to have tried to buy Paine off from publishing the second part of *Rights of Man*. When that failed he hired George Chalmers, an emigrant Maryland Tory, to write a scurrilous popular life of Paine ; for a long time putting down Paine and the Painites was one of the chief domestic concerns of his government. Lady Hester Stanhope is quoted as saying that in those days Pitt used to say to his few intimate friends, "Tom Paine is quite in the right, but what am I to do ? As things are, if I were to encourage Tom Paine's opinions we should have a bloody revolution."

The machinery of outraged prerogative got under way slowly enough to allow Paine to publish and to sell thousands of copies of the second part of *Rights of Man*. The profits he turned over to the Society for Constitutional Information. But Pitt knew his England ; condemnation of Paine and the bloody work of the revolutionary mobs rose in shrill chorus from the gentry and the corporations of the towns and the business men of the cities ; by next Guy Fawkes day, mobs were parading, instead of the heads of the king's pensioners and the owners of rotten boroughs, scarecrows made in the effigy of Thomas Paine and burning them in the market squares. Paine reached Dover and got aboard ship for France just twenty minutes before the officers turned up with a warrant for his arrest. While the customs inspector was searching his trunks on the pier before allowing him to take them aboard the packet, he found and handed back respectfully the polite but uncomfortable letter that Washington had written Paine thanking him for the gift of a package of copies of *Rights of Man*, for which the President obviously felt small enthusiasm, because all he could manage to say was :

And as no one can feel a greater interest in the happiness of mankind than I do, it is the first wish of my heart that the enlightened policy of the present age may diffuse to all men those blessings to which they are entitled and lay the foundation of happiness for future generations.

But the great signature overawed the customs officer so that they let Paine's baggage go. A few months later the courts of the realm had declared him an outlaw, what money he had left had been confiscated, and printers bold enough to print his works were jailed and transported. When a bridge was put across a river in Derbyshire according to Paine's model, very little was said about the name of the designer.

5

Beside Paine on the deck of the packet as the chalk cliffs faded into the September murk stood a certain Citizen Audibert, of Calais, who had come to announce to him his election to the French Convention by three separate departments. In August the National Assembly had conferred honorary French citizenship on Paine, Priestley, Bentham, Washington, Hamilton, Madison, Klopstock, Anacharsis Cloots, and other internationally famous republicans. At Calais the whole town turned out to meet him. He was kissed on both cheeks by officials, appeared at flagdraped balconies, listened

to orations in theatres, was hung with tricolor scarfs,
and presented with cockades by pretty girls all the way
to Paris. There he stopped at White's Hotel, the
American hangout of the time. He had accepted the
seat for the Pas de Calais, and was sworn in at the
Tuileries by the retiring National Assembly with
the rest of the deputies amid the crowds and the parades
and the booming minute-guns of the celebrations of the
first day of the Year One.

Immediately the Convention set to work : royalty
was abolished. Phrases could be made into deeds ;
from the first the Convention was dizzy with power.
The day before, in the engagement at Valmy the revolutionary army under Kellerman had stopped the allies
and émigrés under the Duke of Brunswick and given
the Duke such a scare that he was soon in full retreat
across the Rhine. A few days before that so shrewd an
observer as Gouverneur Morris, then American minister, and like so many American diplomatic representatives in the years to come, a passionate reactionary,
had written Washington to assure him that the allied
armies would have the French monarchy on its feet
again inside of three months. The Revolution of the
World had won its first military victory. But any-
one who hated civil bloodshed as much as Paine must
have felt that in the September massacres, of which he
was probably hearing for the first time, the revolution
in the sense he wanted it, had met its first defeat. No
man ever recognized more pragmatically than Paine
that violence follows its own laws, and that no useful
social order can be founded on massacre. But the forces
at work in Europe were too immense for a few men to
control, even if they had been infinitely more level-
headed than they were ; an entire social order, with all
its ingrained habits, inhibitions, methods of procedure,
was crashing to the ground, leaving in its place only humanitarian phrases, speeches, tricolor cockades. Things

were far different from what they had been in America, where the day the redcoats were driven out of a town, the old habits of local selfgovernment bobbed up, and the frame of institutions was already standing ready to be draped with republican bunting. The French people were starved for power. They had been the prey of generations of oppressions. They were tortured by hatreds, fears, feudal habits of thought no Englishman could understand.

With a quiet courage that is breathtaking when the state of mind in Paris in those autumn months is understood — the day the king was brought back from Varennes, Paine had been almost lynched for an aristocrat because he went out-doors without a tricolor cockade in his hat — he set to work to try to save the king's life. He tried reasonable arguments and the plea that as Louis had befriended the American republic, he should be exiled to America where "remote from the miseries and crimes of royalty, he may learn, from the constant aspect of public prosperity, that the true system of governments consists not in kings, but in fair, equal, and honorable representation." Paine spoke no French, and had no habit of public speaking, so his addresses to the Convention were read in translation by the clerk, while Paine stood quietly beside him in the tribune, probably wearing the same quakerish snuffcolored suit and the oldfashioned bobtailed wig that had so entertained Royall Tyler in London. At the session of January 19, 1793, the day after the news of his outlawry in England had been published in the *Moniteur*, he appeared in the tribune to ask the assembly to reconsider the vote for death. It was with great difficulty that the clerk reading the translation of Paine's statement made his voice heard. Marat shouted that a Quaker, whose religious scruples were opposed to the death penalty, had no right to speak on the subject. When the clerk finished amid indignant yells from the Jacobins, a voice called out that the translation was false. Marat asked Paine some questions in bad English and then announced from the tribune that the translation was a fraud, that these could not be the real sentiments of Thomas Paine, and that anyway a Quaker's opinion was worthless. Brissot and some of the Girondins took courage from Paine's boldness and spoke for commuting the sentence to life imprisonment as a matter of political expediency. They were howled down. The next day the streets around the Tuileries were packed by a mob of tough supporters of the Jacobins from the sections, calling for the king's death, and the death penalty was confirmed. The delirious reign of Queen Guillotine had begun.

Meanwhile the frenzy of the revolution was only matched by the frenzy of the reaction. Burke in England was in correspondence with all the royalist factions and kept dinning the woes of the hapless aristocrats into the ears of parliament. Pitt had the country virtually under martial law. The great coalition of frightened privilege against the republic was building. But meanwhile the French armies were on the march in every direction. In September Montesquieu had taken Savoy from the King of Sardinia. Another army occupied Nice. Dumouriez, the hero of Valmy, entered Brussels in the middle and Antwerp at the end of November. Meanwhile Custine's little army of Alsace was comfortably installed in the rich Rhineland cities of Coblenz, Mainz and Frankfort, proclaiming the rights of man and raising forced loans from the wealthy ; and the Bourbons in Spain and Naples had been compelled, instead of coming to the help of their unfortunate relative, to come to terms with the republic.

In Paris Paine was busy with the committee to which he was elected with Sieyès, Condorcet, Danton, Brissot, Barère and a few others, working up a draft of the constitution that was supposed to be the main business of the Constitutional Convention, but that, in the stress of the factional struggles of the period of the Terror, the Convention never could keep its mind on. Power, direct power now, not Utopia in the future, was what the parties were tearing each other to pieces for.

Meanwhile Paine was living on the Passage des Petits Pères near the oval Place des Victoires, the centre of a group of young English and Irish republicans who were attracted to Paris as the moth to the flame, and of Americans like Joel Barlow, who was there half as a revolutionist and half as agent of a land company. While the Gironde held power, Paine was still highly considered ; he was admired for his outspokenness and for his coolheaded nerve during the hysterical days of the King's trial. The Commune of Paris was the fief of the Jacobins ; Paris would rule the republic one and indivisible; but many of the provincial deputies wanted a federal government modeled on that of the United States, and among them Paine's opinion had weight.

He was appointed a member of the Committee of Surveillance and through that position was able to save the lives of a number of Englishmen who were caught in Paris by the declaration of war in February 1793, and notably of a certain Captain Grimstone of the Royal Artillery, who, swelling up with patriotic fury at a dinner in the garden of the Maison Égalité, punched Paine in the jaw and called him a traitor. The penalty for striking a deputy was death, but Paine managed to get the young man a passport and to smuggle him out of the country. He also managed to make himself useful to the many American seacaptains whose ships were held for contraband in French ports. He was, in fact, the unofficial ambassador of American republicans and British radicals, and that was how he came into conflict with Gouverneur Morris.

If we were not living in a similar period of violent political antagonisms today, it would be hard to under-

stand the virulence of partisan motives even among
Americans at that time and the curious way they in-
teracted with petty jealousies and the great universal
cause of selfinterest. Gouverneur Morris and Paine had
known each other for many years. Although a man
of brains and great personal charm, Morris had all the
snobbery of the Hudson River landowners of the old
Dutch school who considered themselves a special aristocracy equal to any in Europe. He seems to have
fascinated Paine by his bluster and his humor, while
he despised Paine, as you can see by his diary, as an upstart and a social inferior. Morris, starting out as an
American patriot and friend of Washington, had felt
himself very much at home in the boudoir intrigues of
the last days of the old regime and was the sleeping
partner of many a noble lady for whom the events of
1792 were the crack of doom. So in a very exact sense
his heart, and it was much divided, was with the coalition. Then Morris too, like about every other American in Europe at the time, had a landselling scheme ; all
the time he was working for the restoration of the old
regime he was selling virgin forests to the noble hus-
bands of the noble ladies of his choice. A landowner
and Federalist at home, he couldn't help seeing the
agrarian side of the revolution, with its burning of châ-
teaux and suppression of feudal rights and parceling
out of the great estates, as a hideous nightmare. Like
so many Americans since, he soon found himself more
royalist than the king ; it became one of the passions
of his life to keep the revolutionary disease from spreading to America. Personal jealousy also entered in, because, while he was official envoy, it was inevitable that
a great deal of business should be done through Paine,
whom the republicans trusted. It's not surprising that
he did his best to undermine Paine's influence in Paris,
where, as well as carrying on continual intrigue with
the royalists and the agents of Pitt, he had close relations

with the Committee of Public Safety. There's no other explanation, than nods and winks of Morris's in the proper quarters, for the curious note found in Robespierre's papers in Robespierre's own handwriting : "Demand that Thomas Paine be decreed of accusation for the interests of America as much as of France."

After the fall of the Girondins, Paine felt politically powerless and went back to writing. He lived with some English and American friends in an old house that had once belonged to la Pompadour on the rue du Faubourg St. Denis, which he described in a letter to Lady Smyth, the wife of a British banker in Paris, a few years later, after he had become good friends with both Smyths.

They [the lodgings] were the most agreeable, for the situation, of any I ever had in Paris, except that they were too remote from the convention of which I was then a member. But this was recompensed by their being also remote from the alarms and confusions into which the interior of Paris was then often thrown. The news of those things used to arrive to us, as if we were in a state of tranquility in the country.

The house, which was enclosed by a wall and gateway from the street, was a good deal like an old mansion farmhouse, and the courtyard was like a farmyard, stocked with fowls, ducks, turkeys and geese ; which for amusement we used to feed out of the parlor window on the ground floor. There were some hutches for rabbits and a sty with two pigs.

Beyond, was a garden of more than an acre of ground, well laid out and stocked with excellent fruit trees. The orange, apricot and greengage plum, were the best I ever tasted ; and it is the only place where I saw the wild cucumber. The place had formerly been occupied by some curious person.

My apartments consisted of three rooms ; the first for wood, water, etc., with an old fashioned closet chest, high enough to hang up clothes in ; the next was the bed room ; and beyond it the sitting room, which looked into the gar-

den through a glass door ; and on the outside there was a
small landing place railed in, and a flight of narrow stairs
almost hidden by the vines that grew over it, by which I
could descend into the garden without going down stairs
through the house.

[The letter was copied out by Yorke in fragments. The
sections omitted probably referred to some Englishmen or
Americans who were in a jam.]

I went into my chambers to write and sign a certificate
for them, which I intended to take to the guardhouse to
obtain their release. Just as I had finished it a man came
into my room dressed in the Parisian uniform of a captain,
and spoke to me in good English, and with a good address.
He told me that two young men, Englishmen, were arrested and detained in the guard-house, and that the section
(meaning those who represented and acted for the section),
had sent him to ask me if I knew them, in which case they
would be liberated.

This matter being soon settled between us, he talked to
me about the Revolution, and something about the "Rights
of Man," which he had read in English ; and at parting
offered me in a polite and civil manner, his services. And
who do you think the man was that offered me his services?
It was no other than the public executioner Samson, who
guillotined the King, and all who were guillotined in Paris ;
and who lived in the same section, and in the same street
with me. . .

As to myself, I used to find some relief by walking alone
in the garden after dark, and cursing with hearty good will
the authors of that terrible system that had turned the character of the Revolution I had been proud to defend.

I went but little to the Convention, and then only to make
my appearance ; because I found it impossible to join in
their tremendous decrees, and useless and dangerous to oppose them. My having voted and spoken extensively, more
so than any other member, against the execution of the
King, had already fixed a mark upon me : neither dared any
of my associates in the Convention to translate and speak
in French for me anything I might have dared to have
written. . .

Pen and ink were then of no use to me : no good could

be done by writing, and no printer dared to print; and whatever I might have written for my private amusement, as anecdotes of the times, would have been continually exposed to be examined, and tortured into any meaning that the rage of party might fix upon it; and as to softer subjects, my heart was in distress at the fate of my friends, and my harp hung upon the weeping willows.

As it was summer we spent most of our time in the garden, and passed it away in those childish amusements that serve to keep reflection from the mind, such as marbles, scotch-hops, battledores, etc., at which we were all pretty expert.

In this retired manner we remained about six or seven weeks, and our landlord went every evening into the city to bring us the news of the day and the evening journal. . .

[The passage here omitted must have referred to a young Englishman named Johnson, who lived with the group around Paine, and was so upset by the news that Marat was going to bring an accusation against Paine, that he tried to stab himself to death, leaving a will by which Paine was his heir.]

He recovered, and being anxious to get out of France, a passage was obtained for him and Mr. Choppin; they received it late in the evening, and set off the next morning for Basel before four, from which place I had a letter from them, highly pleased with their escape from France, into which they had entered with an enthusiasm of patriotic devotion. Ah, France! thou hast ruined the character of a Revolution virtuously begun, and destroyed those who produced it. I might almost say like Job's servant, "and I, only, am escaped."

Two days after they were gone I heard a rapping at the gate, and looking out of the window of the bed room I saw the landlord going with the candle to the gate, which he opened, and a guard with muskets and fixed bayonets entered. I went to bed again, and made up my mind for prison, for I was then the only lodger. It was a guard to take up [Johnson and Choppin], but, I thank God, they were out of their reach.

The guard came about a month after in the night and took away the landlord Georgeit; and the scene in the house finished with the arrestation of myself. This was soon after you called on me, and sorry I was it was not in my power to render to Sir Robert Smyth the service that you asked. [The service was to get him out of jail.]

When he wrote this Paine must have forgotten that it was during this time that he spent much of each day in his Louis XV boudoir at work on *The Age of Reason*. He described his state of mind under the Terror in a letter written to Samuel Adams in answer to the old revolutionist's denunciation of him for meddling with religion :

My friends were falling as fast as the guillotine could cut their heads off, and as I expected every day the same fate I resolved to begin my work. I appeared to myself to be on my deathbed, for death was on every side of me, and I had no time to lose. This accounts for my writing at the time I did, and so nicely did the time and intention meet, that I had not finished the first part more than six hours before I was arrested and taken to prison. The people of France were running headlong into atheism, and I had the work translated in their own language, to stop them in that career and fix them to the first article of every man's creed, who has a creed at all — *I believe in God*.

On December 28th he was arrested, and his papers were searched. Barlow, who was getting to speak French fluently, acted as interpreter and seems to have managed to convince the guards that there was nothing treasonable among Paine's manuscripts. The guard let Paine turn over his *Age of Reason* to Barlow to take to the printer. Then he was marched off to the Luxembourg, where he spent ten months and very nearly lost his life of prison fever. It seems likely that he escaped the guillotine by an oversight, or else by a trick of Mahraski, the prison doctor, who seems to have been fond of him.

When persons by scores and by hundreds [Paine wrote later] were to be taken out of prison for the guillotine, it was always done in the night, and those who performed that office had a private mark or signal by which they knew what rooms to go to and what number to take. We, as I have said, were four and the door of our room was marked, unobserved by us, with that number in chalk ; but it happened, if happening is the proper word, that the mark was put on when the door was open and flat against the wall, and thereby came on the inside when we shut it at night ; and the destroying angel passed by it.

6

When Paine was dug out of the Luxembourg prison by Monroe in the late fall of 1793 he came out into the talk and clatter of the city — restaurants and cafés and well-dressed people strolling in the open squares and sharp strokes of hoofs of carthorses on cobblestones, and the faint sunlight on the narrow grey misty streets — to find a changed world. The great gale had blown itself out. The survivors of the Convention were meeting at the Tuileries in an atmosphere of exhausted hangover calm. The old regime was gone, but so were the hopes and the moral fervors that were to build the new.

A different race of men had come into being ; the brave men, the honest men, the men willing to sacrifice their own lives for the hope of a new better life for mankind had been taken away in the tumbrils ; gone too was the hysterical ardor of faction of the Mountain and the Gironde. From out of exile and hiding, from out of the crannies and corners of government offices came men like Talleyrand, Fouché, Barras, careerists who would stoop to anything, and had stooped to anything, cynics whose only creed was survive and get ahead. They were crazy for money and power ; they had learned to take no risks. Only the army had been comparatively free of the Terror. Out of the revolutionary fervor of the army, backed in Paris by the Beauharnais gang and his own compact family of greedy

Corsicans, always quarreling among themselves but always ready to make common cause against outsiders, Bonaparte was fashioning the instrument that was to defeat all the petty careerists and cog them into the machinery of the Empire, by which his own career was to be exalted into godhead.

Paine was in very ill health. He was bitterly disillusioned. He had imagined that his friends in America, especially President Washington, would come to his rescue ; Washington had done nothing, and Morris, the president's personal representative, had, Paine thought, helped keep him in jail. In bitterness and sickness his beliefs in an impersonal God and in the nobility of the common man began to harden into religious dogmas. His only appearance at the Convention which invited him back and offered him a pension that he refused, was to read a paper protesting against the projected property restriction on suffrage.

He was taken ill again, and suffered greatly from an abscess in his side and for months was so near dying, that reports of his death were published in England and America, where people received them with joy or sorrow strictly in accord with their partisan feelings.

The Monroes took him to their house and nursed him back to health. After all America was not all Federalist. In fact Washington had been forced to agree to give up Morris, who had been using his diplomatic immunity to cover his business transactions and his every day increasing enthusiasm for the enemies of the French republic. Whether he had hold of enough strings of intrigue in Paris to keep Monroe from being received by the Commissary for Foreign Affairs, or whether (the government was riddled with secrecy, bribery, treason) some other tangle in the Committee of Public Safety was the cause of the delay, is still obscure. Monroe had to appeal directly to the Convention before his credentials as minister were accepted, and Morris, who certainly showed nerve staying in Paris so long as he did when he was already so deeply compromised, fled in a hurry to the Swiss border, following a big shipment of his wines, and rejoined his noble lady-friends in exile. For years after he was busy with the work of reaction in all the courts of the coalition and even wrote proclamations to their loyal subjects for the Bourbons.

The Constitution of the Year III was a sort of afterglow of the Revolution of the World. The Directoire represented the medium landowners and the provincial lawyers and businessmen of France, as Robespierre's Committee of Public Safety had represented the destructive logic and the expanding frenzy of Paris. The royalist reaction was strong in the country, but for a while it seemed as if the Directoire, with all its odd theatrical decorations, would manage to establish a moderate republic based on the liberties of the bill of rights.

Even when the Monroes went back to the States, it was not thought safe for Paine to sail with them, as the British were stopping American ships and searching them and impressing their seamen ; and any British captain of a frigate would have considered Paine, the Outlaw and the Infidel, as good a prize as a Spanish galleon in the old days. So he lived on quietly in Paris, staying with Nicholas de Bonneville and his family. De Bonneville was editor of *La Bouche de Fer*, a republican paper, and a disciple of Paine's. Perhaps it was hard for Paine to tear himself away from Paris, centre of ardent lives and new thoughts, that as fast as it died as a revolutionary capital, came back to life as the theatre of Napoleon's great imperial show.

He filled long columns in the American and French press with his complaints of Washington's neglect, with acute political articles against the Federalists in America and general essays on political economy in France. The essays of this period are of great interest at the present time ; one of them, *Agrarian Justice*, is a foreshadowing of the theories of Henry George and of recent governmental efforts to spread out income.

It's too bad that the excellence of Paine's later journalism has been obscured by the long wrangle over religion that occupied so much of the end of his life. *The Age of Reason* is a work of enthusiastic deism that contrasts the Bible as absolute truth, with the Bible in the light of scientific knowledge and the streetcorner common sense of the time. It is a break with organized religion in the train of thought that led through to unitarianism, Comtian positivism, and such movements as the Ethical Culture Society, that have already sunk into the background of thought of most of the protestant world. The moderate republicans of the Directoire like La Révellière-Lépeaux and the Theophilanthropists felt that the attacks on life and property under the revolutionary tidal wave were partly due to a too rapid loosening of the ethical restraints of organized religion, and were anxious to make a state institution of a reasonable deism, that would be compatible with pragmatic common sense. For a while they held services in Notre Dame. Later Napoleon took the bull by the horns, with a cynical directness thoroughly characteristic of him, and brought back the Roman church, incense, holy water, catechism, confessional and all. But in England and to a certain extent in America, the rising middleclass, led by its clergy, lumped infidelity, the bloodshed of the period of the Terror, and fear of Napoleon into an amalgam of unreasoning hate not quite dissolved to this day. If Paine had written in the language of scholarship, in the small print of theological debate, he would have been tolerated, but he wrote to be read by the people, and the people read him and the only protection British and American churchly institutions had was to turn Paine into the devil himself. Hitler's campaign against the Jews is the modern counterpart in filth and scurrility of the campaign of the respectable people of England against the infidels and the freethinkers. Even today there comes a little whiff of brimstone as you write the two words down. This war without quarter embittered all the later part of Paine's life and kept the republicans in America from getting the full use of his great experience with events and his talents as a political commentator. After all, it's not so long ago that so talented an American as Theodore Roosevelt was referring to Paine as "a dirty little atheist."

It was not until 1802 that he left France. Jefferson had offered him passage home on an American warship. (Jefferson, by the way, never heard the last of it from the godly.) Napoleon's police was making France uncomfortable for republicans and freethinkers, so Paine took with him the wife and children of his friend Bonneville, who hoped to follow later, if he could induce the police to let him go. There's a last glimpse of Paine in Paris in the letters of an English ex-radical Henry Redhead Yorke, who had been cured of radicalism by a prison term in 1795.

Time seemed to have made dreadful ravages over his whole frame, and a settled melancholy was visible on his countenance. He desired me to be seated, and although he did not recollect me for a considerable time, he conversed with his usual affability. I confess I felt extremely surprised that he should have forgotten me ; but I resolved not to make myself known to him, as long as it could be avoided with propriety . . . At length I thought it time to remove his suspence, and stated an incident which instantly recalled me to his mind. It is impossible to describe the sudden change which this effected ; his countenance brightened, he pressed me by the hand, and a silent tear stole down his cheek. Nor was I less affected than himself. For some time we sat without a word escaping from our lips. "Thus we are met once more, Mr. Paine," I resumed, "after a long separation of ten years, and after having been both of us severely weather-beaten." "Aye," he replied, "and who

would have thought that we should meet in Paris ?" He
then enquired what motive had brought me here, and on
my explaining myself, he observed with a smile of contempt, "They have shed blood enough for liberty, and now
they have it in perfection. This is not a country for an
honest man to live in ; they do not understand anything at
all of the principles of free government, and the best way
is to leave them to themselves. You see they have conquered all Europe, only to make it more miserable than it
was before." Upon this, I remarked that I was surprised
to hear him speak in such desponding language of the fortune of mankind, and that I thought much might yet be
done for the Republic. "Republic !" he exclaimed, "do
you call this a Republic ? Why they are worse off than
the slaves of Constantinople ; for there they expect to be
bashaws in heaven by submitting to be slaves below, but
here they believe neither in heaven nor hell, and yet are
slaves by choice. I know of no Republic in the world except America, which is the only country for such men as
you and I. . ."

Paine lived, on the whole, unhappily in America for
seven years. In America, too, there was a change. Everything was on the move. People were straggling
west, opening up new lands ; immigrants were pouring
in from Europe. Rationalism was on the wane ; in its
place was surging up the intolerant violence of evange-
lism in religion and thickskinned business respectability
in ethics. The new generation had little interest in
speculative politics or in generalizations about the good
of mankind. The young people wanted to get rich,
and they were getting rich. Jefferson, Madison, Monroe were landed gentlemen, they were heads of a great
triumphant political party made up of very varied elements. They were a little shocked by Paine's insist-
ence on the religious controversy which seemed to them
beside the point. Of course they agreed with him.
With hardly an exception all American statesmen have
been deists. But religious speculation was something

to talk about among friends after dinner when the darkies had gone back to their quarters, not to write to the papers about. There was always a danger that their rational political plans would be upset if one of them stepped into the hornets' nest of clerical unreason. It was much safer to leave theology to the theologians. Even Joel Barlow, an honest man, and no politician, was upset when Cheetham, who was getting ready his libelous biography of Paine as part of the campaign against Jefferson, wrote asking him for his recollections of his old friend :

Kalorama, Aug. 11. 1809

To James Cheetham, Sir :
    I have received your letter calling for information relative to the life of Thomas Paine. It appears to me that this is not the moment to publish the life of that man in this country. His own writings are his best life, and these are not read at present.
    The greater part of the readers in the United States will not be persuaded, as long as their present feelings last, to consider him in any other light than as a drunkard and a deist. The writer of his life who should dwell on these topics, to the exclusion of the great and estimable traits of his real character, might indeed please the rabble of the age, who do not know him ; the book might sell, but it would only tend to render the truth more obscure for the future biographer than it was before.
    But if the present writer should give us Thomas Paine *complete*, in all his character, as one of the most benevolent and disinterested of mankind, endowed with the clearest perception, an uncommon share of original genius, and the greatest breadth of thought ; if this piece of biography should analyze his literary labors and rank him, as he ought to be ranked, among the brightest and most undeviating luminaries of the age in which he has lived, yet with a mind assailable by flattery, and receiving through that weak side a tincture of vanity which he was too proud to conceal ; with a mind, though strong enough to bear him up and to rise elastic under the heaviest hand of oppression, yet un-

able to endure the contempt of his former friends and
fellow-laborers, the rulers of the country that had received
his first and greatest services ; a mind incapable of looking
down with serene compassion, as it ought, on the rude
scoffs of their imitators, a new generation that knows him
not ; a mind that shrinks from their society, and unhappily
seeks refuge in low company, or looks for consolation in
the sordid, solitary bottle, till it sinks at last so far below its
native elevation as to lose all respect for itself and to forfeit
that of his best friends, disposing these friends almost to
join with his enemies, and wish, though from different
motives, that he would hasten to hide himself in the grave
— if you are disposed and prepared to write his life *thus entire*, to fill up the picture to which these hasty strokes of
outline give but a rude sketch with great vacuities, your
book may be a useful one for another age, but it will not be
relished, nor scarcely tolerated, in this.

The biographer of Thomas Paine should not forget his
mathematical acquirements and his mechanical genius : his
invention of the *iron bridge*, which led him to Europe in
the year 1787, and which has procured him a great reputation in that branch of science in France and England, in
both which countries his bridge has been adopted in many
instances, and is now much in use.

You ask whether he took the oath of allegiance to France.
Doubtless the qualification to be a member of the Convention required an oath of fidelity to that country, but involved in it no abjuration of his fidelity to his. He was
made a French citizen by the same decree with *Washington, Hamilton, Priestley, and Sir James Mackintosh.*

What Mr. M.—— has told you relative to the circumstances of his arrestation by order of Robespierre is er-
roneous, at least in one point. Paine did not lodge at the
house where he was arrested, but had been dining there
with some Americans, of whom Mr. M.—— may have been
one. I never heard before that Paine was intoxicated that
night. Indeed, the officers brought him directly to my
home, which was two miles from his lodging and about as
much from the place where he had been dining. He was
not intoxicated when they came to me. Their object was
to get me to go and assist them to examine Paine's papers.

It employed us the rest of that night and the whole of the next day at Paine's lodgings, and he was not committed to prison till the next evening.

You ask what company he kept. He always frequented the best, both in England and France, till he became the object of calumny in certain American papers (echoes of the English court papers) for his adherence to what he thought the cause of liberty in France — till he conceived himself neglected and despised by his former friends in the United States. From that moment he gave himself very much to drink, and, consequently, to companions less worthy of his better days.

It is said he was always a peevish ingrate. This is possible. So was *Lawrence Sterne,* so was *Torquato Tasso,* so was *J. J. Rousseau.* But Thomas Paine, as a visiting acquaintance and as a literary friend, the only points of view from which I knew him, was one of the most instructive men I have ever known. He had a surprising memory and a brilliant fancy ; his mind was a storehouse of facts and useful observations ; he was full of lively anecdote and ingenious, original, pertinent remarks upon almost every subject.

He was always charitable to the poor beyond his means, a sure protector and friend to all Americans in distress that he found in foreign countries. And he had frequent occasions to exert his influence in protecting them during the revolution in France. His writings will answer for his patriotism, and his entire devotion to what he conceived to be the best interest and happiness of mankind.

This, sir, is all I have to remark on the subject you mention. Now I have only one request to make, and that would doubtless seem impertinent were you not the editor of a newspaper ; it is, that you will not publish this letter, nor permit a copy of it to be taken.

JOEL BARLOW

Cheetham himself had met Paine and wrote this ungracious but vivid account of the meeting :

After his return to the United States from France I became acquainted with him on his arrival at New-York, in the year 1802. He introduced himself to me by letter from Washington City, requesting me to take lodgings for him in New-York. I accordingly engaged a room for him in Lovett's Hotel, supposing him to be a gentleman, and apprised him of the number. On his arrival, about ten at night, he wrote me a note desiring to see me immediately. I waited on him at Lovett's in company with Mr. George Clinton, Jun. We rapped at the door : a small figure opened it within, meanly dressed, having on an old top coat without an under one ; a dirty silk handkerchief loosely thrown around his neck ; a long beard of more than a week's growth ; a face well carbuncled, fiery as the setting sun, and the whole figure staggering under a load of inebriation. I was on the point of enquiring for Mr. Paine, when I saw in his countenance something of the portraits I had seen of him. We were desired to be seated. He had before him a small round table, on which were a beefstake, some beer, a pint of brandy, a pitcher of water and a glass. He sat eating, drinking, talking with as much composure as if he had lived with us all his life.

In his last years Paine was much persecuted by the godly. His fellowtownsmen at New Rochelle refused to let him vote, claiming that he was not an American citizen. While he was dying, in a little house on what is now Grove Street in New York, a story is told that a Catholic priest and a Protestant minister, and a pious old lady broke in succession into his bedroom to exhort him to repent. The Quakers refused him burial in their burying ground. Even after he was dead and buried on his farm in New Rochelle, his bones were not allowed to rest quiet. William Cobbett, who from a violent antagonist had been turned into a violent partisan of Paine's by reading his essay on Pitt's financial system, dug up his bones and carried them to England where he intended to give them a state funeral, but found the reaction against infidelity and republicanism still too strong. Even the town crier who announced the arrival of Tom Paine's bones was arrested. Years later the bones were seized with the rest of Cobbett's effects when he went into bankruptcy. The Lord Chancellor refused to regard them as an asset and they were given to an old daylaborer who carted them off no one knows where. Years later the coffin turned up at a second-hand dealer's in London. The trunk containing Paine's manuscript notes and correspondence and, possibly, an autobiography, which was inherited by Mme. de Bonneville, who turned Catholic after her husband's death and tried to forget her libertarian past, was lost in the burning of a warehouse belonging to one of her sons in St. Louis in the middle of the last century. As Joel Barlow said, his writings are his life.

John Dos Passos has selected
the essence of Tom Paine's thought from

COMMON SENSE
THE AMERICAN CRISIS
RIGHTS OF MAN
AGRARIAN JUSTICE
LETTERS TO *The National Intelligencer*

THE MOST IMPORTANT WORKS OF

THOMAS PAINE

(1737–1809)

Common Sense (1776)
The American Crisis (1776–1783)
Rights of Man, Parts I and II (1791–1792)
Age of Reason, Parts I and II (1794–1795)
Dissertation on First Principles of Government (1795)
Decline and Fall of the English System of Finance
(1796)
Agrarian Justice (1797)

COMMON SENSE

(1776)

Some writers have so confounded society with government, as to leave little or no distinction between them ; whereas they are not only different, but have different origins. Society is produced by our wants and government by our wickedness ; the former promotes our happiness *positively* by uniting our affections, the latter *negatively* by restraining our vices. The one encourages intercourse, the other creates distinctions. The first is a patron, the last a punisher.

Society in every state is a blessing, but government, even in its best state, is but a necessary evil ; in its worst state an intolerable one : for when we suffer, or are exposed to the same miseries *by a government*, which we might expect in a country *without government*, our calamity is heightened by reflecting that we furnish the means by which we suffer. Government, like dress, is the badge of lost innocence ; the palaces of kings are built upon the ruins of the bowers of paradise. For were the impulses of conscience clear, uniform and irresistibly obeyed, man would need no other lawgiver ; but that not being the case, he finds it necessary to surrender up a part of his property to furnish means for the protection of the rest ; and this he is induced to do by the same prudence which in every other case advises him, out of two evils to choose the least. Wherefore, security being the true design and end of government, it unanswerably follows that whatever form thereof appears most likely to ensure it to us, with the least expence and greatest benefit, is preferable to all others.

In order to gain a clear and just idea of the design

and end of government, let us suppose a small number
of persons settled in some sequestered part of the earth,
unconnected with the rest ; they will then represent
the first peopling of any country, or of the world.   In
this state of natural liberty, society will be their first
thought. A thousand motives will excite them thereto ;
the strength of one man is so unequal to his wants,
and his mind so unfitted for perpetual solitude, that
he is soon obliged to seek assistance and relief of another, who in his turn requires the same.   Four or
five united would be able to raise a tolerable dwelling
in the midst of a wilderness, but one man might labor
out the common period of life without accomplishing
any thing ; when he had felled his timber he could not
remove it, nor erect it after it was removed ; hunger
in the mean time would urge him to quit his work, and
every different want would call him a different way.
Disease, nay even misfortune, would be death ; for
though neither might be mortal, yet either would disable him from living, and reduce him to a state in which
he might rather be said to perish than to die.

Thus necessity, like a gravitating power, would soon
form our newly arrived emigrants into society, the
reciprocal blessings of which would supercede, and
render the obligations of law and government unnecessary while they remained perfectly just to each other ;
but as nothing but Heaven is impregnable to vice, it
will unavoidably happen that in proportion as they surmount the first difficulties of emigration, which bound
them together in a common cause, they will begin to
relax in their duty and attachment to each other : and
this remissness will point out the necessity of establishing some form of government to supply the defect of
moral virtue.

Some convenient tree will afford them a State House,
under the branches of which the whole colony may

assemble to deliberate on public matters. It is more than probable that their first laws will have the title only of regulations and be enforced by no other penalty than public disesteem. In this first parliament every man by natural right will have a seat.

But as the colony increases, the public concerns will increase likewise, and the distance at which the members may be separated, will render it too inconvenient for all of them to meet on every occasion as at first, when their number was small, their habitations near, and the public concerns few and trifling. This will point out the convenience of their consenting to leave the legislative part to be managed by a select number chosen from the whole body, who are supposed to have the same concerns at stake which those have who appointed them, and who will act in the same manner as the whole body would act were they present. If the colony continue increasing, it will become necessary to augment the number of representatives, and that the interest of every part of the colony may be attended to, it will be found best to divide the whole into convenient parts, each part sending its proper number : and that the *elected* might never form to themselves an interest separate from the *electors*, prudence will point out the propriety of having elections often : because as the *elected* might by that means return and mix again with the general body of the *electors* in a few months, their fidelity to the public will be secured by the prudent reflection of not making a rod for themselves. And as this frequent interchange will establish a common interest with every part of the community, they will mutually and naturally support each other, and on this, (not on the unmeaning name of king,) depends the *strength of government, and the happiness of the governed*.

Here then is the origin and rise of government;

namely, a mode rendered necessary by the inability of moral virtue to govern the world ; here too is the design and end of government, viz. freedom and security. And however our eyes may be dazzled with show, or our ears deceived by sound ; however prejudice may warp our wills, or interest darken our understanding, the simple voice of nature and reason will say, 'tis right.

I draw my idea of the form of government from a principle in nature which no art can overturn, viz. that the more simple any thing is, the less liable it is to be disordered, and the easier repaired when disordered ; and with this maxim in view I offer a few remarks on the so much boasted Constitution of England. That it was noble for the dark and slavish times in which it was erected, is granted. When the world was overrun with tyranny the least remove therefrom was a glorious rescue. But that it is imperfect, subject to convulsions, and incapable of producing what it seems to promise, is easily demonstrated.

Absolute governments, (though the disgrace of human nature) have this advantage with them, they are simple ; if the people suffer, they know the head from which their suffering springs ; know likewise the remedy ; and are not bewildered by a variety of causes and cures. But the Constitution of England is so exceedingly complex, that the nation may suffer for years together without being able to discover in which part the fault lies ; some will say in one and some in another, and every political physician will advise a different medicine.

I know it is difficult to get over local or long standing prejudices, yet if we will suffer ourselves to examine the component parts of the English Constitution, we shall find them to be the base remains of two ancient tyrannies, compounded with some new Republican materials.

First — The remains of monarchical tyranny in the person of the king.

Secondly — The remains of aristocratical tyranny in the persons of the peers.

Thirdly — The new Republican materials, in the persons of the Commons, on whose virtue depends the freedom of England.

The two first, by being hereditary, are independent of the people ; wherefore in a *constitutional sense* they contribute nothing towards the freedom of the State.

To say that the Constitution of England is an *union* of three powers, reciprocally *checking* each other, is farcical ; either the words have no meaning, or they are flat contradictions.

To say that the Commons is a check upon the king, presupposes two things.

First — That the king is not to be trusted without being looked after ; or in other words, that a thirst for absolute power is the natural disease of monarchy.

Secondly — That the Commons, by being appointed for that purpose, are either wiser or more worthy of confidence than the crown.

But as the same constitution which gives the Commons a power to check the king by withholding the supplies, gives afterwards the king a power to check the Commons, by empowering him to reject their other bills ; it again supposes that the king is wiser than those whom it has already supposed to be wiser than him. A mere absurdity !

Mankind being originally equals in the order of creation, the equality could only be destroyed by some subsequent circumstance : the distinctions of rich and poor may in a great measure be accounted for, and that without having recourse to the harsh ill-sounding names of oppression and avarice. Oppression is often the *consequence*, but seldom or never the *means* of riches; and though avarice will preserve a man from being necessitously poor, it generally makes him too timorous to be wealthy.

But there is another and greater distinction for which no truly natural or religious reason can be assigned, and that is the distinction of men into KINGS and SUBJECTS. Male and female are the distinctions of nature, good and bad the distinctions of heaven; but how a race of men came into the world so exalted above the rest, and distinguished like some new species, is worth inquiring into, and whether they are the means of happiness or of misery to mankind.

In the early ages of the world, according to the scripture chronology there were no kings; the consequence of which was, there were no wars; it is the pride of kings which throws mankind into confusion. Holland, without a king hath enjoyed more peace for this last century than any of the monarchical governments in Europe. Antiquity favors the same remark; for the quiet and rural lives of the first Patriarchs have a happy something in them, which vanishes when we come to the history of Jewish royalty.

Government by kings was first introduced into the world by the heathens, from whom the children of Israel copied the custom. It was the most prosperous invention the devil ever set on foot for the promotion of idolatry. The heathens paid divine honors to their deceased kings, and the Christian world has improved on the plan by doing the same to their living ones. How impious is the title of sacred majesty applied to a worm, who in the midst of his splendor is crumbling into dust!

To the evil of monarchy we have added that of hereditary succession; and as the first is a degradation and lessening of ourselves, so the second, claimed as a matter of right, is an insult and imposition on posterity. For all men being originally equals, no one by birth

could have a right to set up his own family in perpetual
preference to all others for ever, and though himself
might deserve some decent degree of honors of his
contemporaries, yet his descendants might be far too unworthy to inherit them. One of the strongest natural
proofs of the folly of hereditary right in kings, is that
nature disapproves it, otherwise she would not so frequently turn it into ridicule, by giving mankind an
ass for a lion.

Secondly, as no man at first could possess any other
public honors than were bestowed upon him, so the
givers of those honors could have no power to give
away the right of posterity, and though they might
say "We choose you for our head," they could not
without manifest injustice to their children say "that
your children and your children's children shall reign
over ours for ever." Because such an unwise, unjust,
unnatural compact might (perhaps) in the next succession put them under the government of a rogue or
a fool. Most wise men in their private sentiments have
ever treated hereditary right with contempt; yet it
is one of those evils which when once established is
not easily removed: many submit from fear, others
from superstition, and the more powerful part shares
with the king the plunder of the rest.

This is supposing the present race of kings in the
world to have had an honorable origin: whereas it is
more than probable, that, could we take off the dark
covering of antiquity and trace them to their first rise,
we should find the first of them nothing better than
the principal ruffian of some restless gang; whose
savage manners or pre-eminence in subtilty obtained
him the title of chief among plunderers: and who by
increasing in power and extending his depredations,
overawed the quiet and defenceless to purchase their
safety by frequent contributions. Yet his electors
could have no idea of giving hereditary right to his

descendants, because such a perpetual exclusion of themselves was incompatible with the free and unrestrained principles they professed to live by. Wherefore, hereditary succession in the early ages of monarchy could not take place as a matter of claim, but as something casual or complemental ; but as few or no records were extant in those days, and traditionary history stuff'd with fables, it was very easy, after the lapse of a few generations, to trump up some superstitious tale conveniently timed, Mahomet-like, to cram hereditary right down the throats of the vulgar. Perhaps the disorders which threatened, or seemed to threaten, on the decease of a leader and the choice of a new one (for elections among ruffians could not be very orderly) induced many at first to favor hereditary pretensions ; by which means it happened, as it hath happened since, that what at first was submitted to as a convenience was afterwards claimed as a right.

England since the conquest hath known some few good monarchs, but groaned beneath a much larger number of bad ones ; yet no man in his senses can say that their claim under William the Conqueror is a very honorable one. A French bastard landing with armed banditti and establishing himself king of England against the consent of the natives, is in plain terms a very paltry rascally original. It certainly hath no divinity in it. However it is needless to spend much time in exposing the folly of hereditary right ; if there are any so weak as to believe it, let them promiscuously worship the ass and the lion, and welcome. I shall neither copy their humility, nor disturb their devotion.

Yet I should be glad to ask how they suppose kings came at first ? The question admits but of three answers, viz. either by lot, by election, or by usurpation. If the first king was taken by lot, it establishes a precedent for the next, which excludes hereditary succession. Saul was by lot, yet the succession was

not hereditary, neither does it appear from that trans-
action that there was any intention it ever should. If
the first king of any country was by election, that likewise establishes a precedent for the next ; for to say,
that the right of all future generations is taken away,
by the act of the first electors, in their choice not only
of a king but of a family of kings for ever, hath no
parallel in or out of scripture but the doctrine of original sin, which supposes the free will of all men lost in
Adam ; and from such comparison, and it will admit
of no other, hereditary succession can derive no glory.
For as in Adam all sinned, and as in the first electors all
men obeyed ; as in the one all mankind were subjected
to Satan, and in the other to sovereignty ; as our innocence was lost in the first, and our authority in the
last ; and as both disable us from reassuming some
former state and privilege, it unanswerably follows that
original sin and hereditary succession are parallels.
Dishonorable rank ! inglorious connection ! yet the
most subtle sophist cannot produce a juster simile.

If we inquire into the business of a king, we shall
find that in some countries they may have none ; and
after sauntering away their lives without pleasure to
themselves or advantage to the nation, withdraw from
the scene, and leave their successors to tread the same
idle round.   In absolute monarchies the whole weight
of business civil and military lies on the king ; the
children of Israel in their request for a king urged this
plea, "that he may judge us, and go out before us and
fight our battles."   But in countries where he is neither
a judge nor a general, as in England, a man would be
puzzled to know what *is* his business.

The nearer any government approaches to a Republic, the less business there is for a king.   It is somewhat difficult to find a proper name for the government of England.   Sir William Meredith calls it a
Republic ; but in its present state it is unworthy of the

name, because the corrupt influence of the crown,
by having all the places in its disposal, hath so effectually swallowed up the power, and eaten out the virtue
of the House of Commons (the republican part in the
Constitution) that the government of England is nearly
as monarchical as that of France or Spain. Men fall
out with names without understanding them. For 'tis
the republican and not the monarchical part of the
Constitution of England which Englishmen glory in,
viz. the liberty of choosing an House of Commons
from out of their own body — and it is easy to see that
when republican virtues fail, slavery ensues. Why is
the Constitution of England sickly, but because monarchy hath poisoned the Republic; the crown has engrossed the Commons.

In England a king hath little more to do than to make
war and give away places; which, in plain terms, is to
empoverish the nation and set it together by the ears.
A pretty business indeed for a man to be allowed eight
hundred thousand sterling a year for, and worshipped
into the bargain! Of more worth is one honest man
to society, and in the sight of God, than all the
crowned ruffians that ever lived.

In the following pages I offer nothing more than
simple facts, plain arguments, and common sense:
and have no other preliminaries to settle with the
reader, than that he will divest himself of prejudice
and prepossession, and suffer his reason and his feelings
to determine for themselves: that he will put on, or
rather that he will not put off, the true character of a
man, and generously enlarge his views beyond the
present day.

Volumes have been written on the subject of the
struggle between England and America. Men of all
ranks have embarked in the controversy, from different
motives, and with various designs; but all have been

ineffectual, and the period of debate is closed. Arms as the last resource decide the contest; the appeal was the choice of the king, and the continent has accepted the challenge.

It hath been reported of the late Mr. Pelham (who though an able minister was not without his faults) that on his being attacked in the House of Commons on the score that his measures were only of a temporary kind, replied, "*they will last my time.*" Should a thought so fatal and unmanly possess the colonies in the present contest, the name of ancestors will be remembered by future generations with detestation.

The sun never shone on a cause of greater worth. 'Tis not the affair of a city, a county, a province, or a kingdom; but of a continent — of at least one eighth part of the habitable globe. 'Tis not the concern of a day, a year, or an age; posterity are virtually involved in the contest, and will be more or less affected even to the end of time, by the proceedings now. Now is the seed-time of continental union, faith and honor. The least fracture now will be like a name engraved with the point of a pin on the tender rind of a young oak; the wound would enlarge with the tree, and posterity read it in full grown characters.

By referring the matter from argument to arms, a new era for politics is struck — a new method of thinkings has arisen. All plans, proposals, &c. prior to the nineteenth of April, *i.e.* to the commencement of hostilities, are like the almanacks of the last year; which though proper then, are superceded and useless now. Whatever was advanced by the advocates on either side of the question then, terminated in one and the same point, viz. a union with Great Britain; the only difference between the parties was the method of effecting it; the one proposing force, the other friendship; but it has so far happened that the first has failed, and the second has withdrawn her influence.

As much has been said of the advantages of reconciliation, which, like an agreeable dream, has passed away and left us as we were, it is but right that we should examine the contrary side of the argument, and inquire into some of the many material injuries which these colonies sustain, and always will sustain, by being connected with and dependent on Great Britain. To examine that connection and dependence, on the principles of nature and common sense, to see what we have to trust to, if separated, and what we are to expect, if dependent.

I have heard it asserted by some, that as America has flourished under her former connection with Great Britain, the same connection is necessary towards her future happiness, and will always have the same effect. Nothing can be more fallacious than this kind of argument. We may as well assert that because a child has thrived upon milk, that it is never to have meat, or that the first twenty years of our lives is to become a precedent for the next twenty. But even this is admitting more than is true ; for I answer roundly, that America would have flourished as much, and probably much more, had no European power taken any notice of her. The commerce by which she hath enriched herself are the necessaries of life, and will always have a market while eating is the custom of Europe.

But she has protected us, say some. That she hath engrossed us is true, and defended the continent at our expense as well as her own, is admitted ; and she would have defended Turkey from the same motive, *viz.* for the sake of trade and dominion.

Alas ! we have been long led away by ancient prejudices and made large sacrifices to superstition. We have boasted the protection of Great Britain, without considering, that her motive was *interest* not *attachment* ; and that she did not protect us from *our enemies* on *our account* ; but from *her enemies* on *her own ac-*

count, from those who had no quarrel with us on any *other account*, and who will always be our enemies on the *same account*. Let Britain waive her pretensions to the continent, or the continent throw off the dependence, and we should be at peace with France and Spain, were they at war with Britain. The miseries of Hanover's last war ought to warn us against connections.

It hath lately been asserted in Parliament, that the colonies have no relation to each other but through the parent country, *i.e.* that Pennsylvania and the Jerseys, and so on for the rest, are sister colonies by the way of England ; this is certainly a very roundabout way of proving relationship, but it is the nearest and only true way of proving enmity (or enemyship, if I may so call it.) France and Spain never were, nor perhaps ever will be, our enemies as *Americans*, but as our being the *subjects of Great Britain.*

But Britain is the parent country, say some. Then the more shame upon her conduct. Even brutes do not devour their young, nor savages make war upon their families ; wherefore, the assertion, if true, turns to her reproach ; but it happens not to be true, or only partly so, and the phrase *parent* or *mother country* hath been jesuitically adopted by the king and his parasites, with a low papistical design of gaining an unfair bias on the credulous weakness of our minds. Europe, and not England, is the parent country of America. This new world hath been the asylum for the persecuted lovers of civil and religious liberty from *every part* of Europe. Hither have they fled, not from the tender embraces of the mother, but from the cruelty of the monster ; and it is so far true of England, that the same tyranny which drove the first emigrants from home, pursues their descendants still.

In this extensive quarter of the globe, we forget the narrow limits of three hundred and sixty miles (the

extent of England) and carry our friendship on a larger
scale ; we claim brotherhood with every European
Christian, and triumph in the generosity of the sentiment.

It is pleasant to observe by what regular gradations
we surmount the force of local prejudices, as we enlarge our acquaintance with the world. A man born in
any town in England divided into parishes, will naturally associate most with his fellow parishioners (because their interests in many cases will be common)
and distinguish him by the name of *neighbor* ; if he
meet him but a few miles from home, he drops the
narrow idea of a street, and salutes him by the name
of *townsman* ; if he travel out of the county and
meet him in any other, he forgets the minor divisions
of street and town, and calls him *countryman, i.e.
countyman* ; but if in their foreign excursions they
should associate in France, or any other part of *Europe,*
their local remembrance would be enlarged into that of
Englishman. And by a just parity of reasoning, all
Europeans meeting in America, or any other quarter
of the globe, are *countrymen* ; for England, Holland,
Germany, or Sweden, when compared with the whole,
stand in the same places on the larger scale, which the
divisions of street, town, and county do on the smaller
ones ; distinctions too limited for continental minds.
Not one third of the inhabitants, even of this province,
[Pennsylvania], are of English descent. Wherefore,
I reprobate the phrase of parent or mother country
applied to England only, as being false, selfish, narrow
and ungenerous.

But, admitting that we were all of English descent,
what does it amount to ? Nothing. Britain, being
now an open enemy, extinguishes every other name
and title : and to say that reconciliation is our duty, is
truly farcical. The first king of England, of the
present line (William the Conqueror) was a French-

man, and half the peers of England are descendants from the same country; wherefore, by the same method of reasoning, England ought to be governed by France.

Much hath been said of the united strength of Britain and the colonies, that in conjunction they might bid defiance to the world. But this is mere presumption; the fate of war is uncertain, neither do the expressions mean any thing; for this continent would never suffer itself to be drained of inhabitants, to support the British arms in either Asia, Africa or Europe.

Besides, what have we to do with setting the world at defiance? Our plan is commerce, and that, well attended to, will secure us the peace and friendship of all Europe; because it is the interest of all Europe to have America a free port. Her trade will aways be a protection, and her barrenness of gold and silver secure her from invaders.

I challenge the warmest advocate for reconciliation to show a single advantage that this continent can reap by being connected with Great Britain. I repeat the challenge; not a single advantage is derived. Our corn will fetch its price in any market in Europe, and our imported goods must be paid for, buy them where we will.

But the injuries and disadvantages which we sustain by that connection, are without number; and our duty to mankind at large, as well as to ourselves, instruct us to renounce the alliance: because, any submission to, or dependence on, Great Britain, tends directly to involve this continent in European wars and quarrels, and set us at variance with nations who would otherwise seek our friendship, and against whom we have neither anger nor complaint. As Europe is our market for trade, we ought to form no partial connection with any part of it. It is the true interest of America to steer clear of European contentions, which she never can do, while, by her dependence on Britain, she is made the make-weight in the scale of British politics.

Europe is too thickly planted with kingdoms to be long at peace, and whenever a war breaks out between England and any foreign power, the trade of America goes to ruin, *because of her connection with Britain.* The next war may not turn out like the last, and should it not, the advocates for reconciliation now will be wishing for separation then, because neutrality in that case would be a safer convoy than a man of war. Every thing that is right or reasonable pleads for separation. The blood of the slain, the weeping voice of nature cries, 'TIS TIME TO PART. Even the distance at which the Almighty hath placed England and America is a strong and natural proof that the authority of the one over the other, was never the design of heaven. The time likewise at which the continent was discovered, adds weight to the argument, and the manner in which it was peopled, encreases the force of it. The Reformation was preceded by the discovery of America : As if the Almighty graciously meant to open a sanctuary to the persecuted in future years, when home should afford neither friendship nor safety.

The authority of Great Britain over this continent, is a form of government, which sooner or later must have an end. And a serious mind can draw no true pleasure by looking forward, under the painful and positive conviction that what he calls "the present constitution" is merely temporary. As parents, we can have no joy, knowing that this government is not sufficiently lasting to insure any thing which we may bequeath to posterity. And by a plain method of argument, as we are running the next generation into debt, we ought to do the work of it, otherwise we use them meanly and pitifully. In order to discover the line of our duty rightly, we should take our children in our hand, and fix our station a few years farther into life ;

that eminence will present a prospect which a few present fears and prejudices conceal from our sight.

Though I would carefully avoid giving unnecessary offence, yet I am inclined to believe, that all those who espouse the doctrine of reconciliation, may be included within the following descriptions.

Interested men, who are not to be trusted, weak men who *cannot* see, prejudiced men who will not see, and a certain set of moderate men who think better of the European world than it deserves ; and this last class, by an ill-judged deliberation, will be the cause of more calamities to this continent than all the other three.

It is the good fortune of many to live distant from the scene of present sorrow ; the evil is not sufficiently brought to their doors to make them feel the precariousness with which all American property is possessed. But let our imaginations transport us a few moments to Boston ; that seat of wretchedness will teach us wisdom, and instruct us for ever to renounce a power in whom we can have no trust. The inhabitants of that unfortunate city who but a few months ago were in ease and affluence, have now no other alternative than to stay and starve, or turn out to beg. Endangered by the fire of their friends if they continue within the city, and plundered by the soldiery if they leave it, in their present situation they are prisoners without the hope of redemption, and in a general attack for their relief they would be exposed to the fury of both armies.

Men of passive tempers look somewhat lightly over the offences of Great Britain, and, still hoping for the best, are apt to call out, *Come, come, we shall be friends again for all this.* But examine the passions and feelings of mankind : bring the doctrine of reconciliation to the touchstone of nature, and then tell me whether you can hereafter love, honor, and faithfully serve the power that hath carried fire and sword into your land? If you cannot do all these, then are you only deceiving yourselves, and by your delay bringing ruin upon posterity. Your future connection with Britain, whom you can neither love nor honor, will be forced and unnatural, and being formed only on the plan of present convenience, will in a little time fall into a relapse more wretched than the first. But if you say, you can still pass the violations over, then I ask, hath your house been burnt? Hath your property been destroyed before your face? Are your wife and children destitute of a bed to lie on, or bread to live on? Have you lost a parent or a child by their hands, and yourself the ruined and wretched survivor? If you have not, then are you not a judge of those who have. But if you have, and can still shake hands with the murderers, then are you unworthy the name of husband, father, friend, or lover, and whatever may be your rank or title in life, you have the heart of a coward, and the spirit of a sycophant.

This is not inflaming or exaggerating matters, but trying them by those feelings and affections which nature justifies, and without which we should be incapable of discharging the social duties of life, or enjoying the felicities of it. I mean not to exhibit horror for the purpose of provoking revenge, but to awaken us from fatal and unmanly slumbers, that we may pursue determinately some fixed object. 'Tis not in the power of Britain or of Europe to conquer America, if she doth not conquer herself by delay and timidity. The present winter is worth an age if rightly employed, but if lost or neglected the whole continent will partake of the misfortune; and there is no punishment which that man doth not deserve, be he who, or what, or where he will, that may be the means of sacrificing a season so precious and useful.

'Tis repugnant to reason, to the universal order of things, to all examples from former ages, to suppose that this continent can long remain subject to any external power. The most sanguine in Britain doth not think so. The utmost stretch of human wisdom cannot, at this time, compass a plan, short of separation, which can promise the continent even a year's security. Reconciliation is *now* a fallacious dream. Nature has deserted the connection, and art cannot supply her place. For, as Milton wisely expresses, "never can true reconcilement grow where wounds of deadly hate have pierced so deep."

Every quiet method for peace hath been ineffectual. Our prayers have been rejected with disdain ; and hath tended to convince us that nothing flatters vanity or confirms obstinacy in kings more than repeated petitioning — and nothing hath contributed more than that very measure to make the kings of Europe absolute. Witness Denmark and Sweden. Wherefore, since nothing but blows will do, for God's sake let us come to a final separation, and not leave the next generation to be cutting throats under the violated unmeaning names of parent and child.

To say they will never attempt it again is idle and visionary ; we thought so at the repeal of the Stamp Act, yet a year or two undeceived us ; as well may we suppose that nations which have been once defeated will never renew the quarrel.

As to government matters, 'tis not in the power of Britain to do this continent justice : the business of it will soon be too weighty and intricate to be managed with any tolerable degree of convenience, by a power so distant from us, and so very ignorant of us ; for if they cannot conquer us, they cannot govern us. To be always running three or four thousand miles with a tale or a petition, waiting four or five months for an answer, which, when obtained, requires five or six more to explain it in, will in a few years be looked upon as folly and childishness. There was a time when it was proper, and there is a proper time for it to cease.

Small islands not capable of protecting themselves are the proper objects for kingdoms to take under their care ; but there is something absurd, in supposing a Continent to be perpetually governed by an island. In no instance hath nature made the satellite larger than its primary planet ; and as England and America, with respect to each other, reverse the common order of nature, it is evident that they belong to different systems. England to Europe : America to itself.

I am not induced by motives of pride, party or resentment to espouse the doctrine of separation and independence ; I am clearly, positively, and conscientiously persuaded that it is the true interest of this continent to be so ; that everything short of *that* is mere patchwork, that it can afford no lasting felicity, — that it is leaving the sword to our children, and shrinking back at a time when a little more, a little further, would have rendered this continent the glory of the earth.

As Britain hath not manifested the least inclination towards a compromise, we may be assured that no terms can be obtained worthy the acceptance of the continent, or any ways equal to the expence of blood and treasure we have been already put to.

The object contended for, ought always to bear some just proportion to the expence. The removal of North, or the whole detestable junto, is a matter unworthy the millions we have expended. A temporary stoppage of trade was an inconvenience, which would have sufficiently balanced the repeal of all the acts complained of, had such repeals been obtained ; but if the whole continent must take up arms, if every man must be a soldier, 'tis scarcely worth our while to fight against a contemptible ministry only. Dearly, dearly do we pay for the repeal of the acts, if that is all we fight for ; for, in a just estimation 'tis as great a folly to pay a Bunker Hill price for law as for land. As I have always considered the independency of this continent, as an event which sooner or later must arrive, so from the late rapid progress of the continent to maturity, the event cannot be far off. Wherefore, on the breaking out of hostilities, it was not worth the while to have disputed a matter which time would have finally redressed, unless we meant to be in earnest : otherwise it is like wasting an estate on a suit at law, to regulate the trespasses of a tenant whose lease is just expiring. No man was a warmer wisher for a reconciliation than myself, before the fatal nineteenth of April 1775, but the moment the event of that day was made known, I rejected the hardened, sullen-tempered Pharaoh of England for ever ; and disdain the wretch, that with the pretended title of FATHER OF HIS PEOPLE can unfeelingly hear of their slaughter, and composedly sleep with their blood upon his soul.

A government of our own is our natural right : and when a man seriously reflects on the precariousness of human affairs, he will become convinced, that it is infinitely wiser and safer, to form a Constitution of our own in a cool deliberate manner, while we have it in our power, than to trust such an interesting event to time and chance. If we omit it now, some Massanello may hereafter arise, who, laying hold of popular disquietudes, may collect together the desperate and the discontented, and by assuming to themselves the powers of government, finally sweep away the liberties of the continent like a deluge. Should the government of America return again into the hands of Britain, the tottering situation of things will be a temptation for some desperate adventurer to try his fortune ; and in such a case, what relief can Britain give ? Ere she could hear the news, the fatal business might be done ; and ourselves suffering like the wretched Britons under the oppression of the conqueror. Ye that oppose independence now, ye know not what ye do : ye are opening a door to eternal tyranny, by keeping vacant the seat of government. There are thousands and tens of thousands, who would think it glorious to expel from the continent, that barbarous and hellish power, which hath stirred up the indians and the negroes to destroy us ; the cruelty hath a double guilt, it is dealing brutally by us, and treacherously by them.

To talk of friendship with those in whom our reason forbids us to have faith, and our affections wounded through a thousand pores instruct us to detest, is madness and folly. Every day wears out the little remains of kindred between us and them ; and can there be any reason to hope, that as the relationship expires, the affection will increase, or that we shall agree better when we have ten times more and greater concerns to quarrel over than ever ?

Ye that tell us of harmony and reconciliation, can ye restore to us the time that is past ? Can ye give to prostitution its former innocence ? neither can ye reconcile Britain and America. The last cord now is broken, the people of England are presenting addresses against us. There are injuries which nature cannot forgive ; she would cease to be nature if she did. As well can the lover forgive the ravisher of his mistress, as the continent forgive the murders of Britain. The Almighty hath implanted in us these unextinguishable feelings for good and wise purposes. They are the guardians of his image in our hearts. They distinguish us from the herd of common animals. The social compact would dissolve, and justice be extirpated from the earth, or have only a casual existence were we callous to the touches of affection. The robber and the murderer would often escape unpunished, did not the injuries which our tempers sustain, provoke us into justice.

O ! ye that love mankind ! Ye that dare oppose not

only the tyranny but the tyrant, stand forth! Every spot of the old world is overrun with oppression. Freedom hath been hunted round the globe. Asia and Africa have long expelled her. Europe regards her like a stranger, and England hath given her warning to depart. O! receive the fugitive, and prepare in time an asylum for mankind.

I have never met with a man, either in England or America, who hath not confessed his opinion, that a separation between the countries would take place one time or other. And there is no instance in which we have shown less judgment, than in endeavoring to describe, what we call, the ripeness or fitness of the continent for independence.

As all men allow the measure, and vary only in their opinion of the time, let us, in order to remove mistakes, take a general survey of things, and endeavor if possible to find out the *very* time. But I need not go far, the inquiry ceases at once, for the *time hath found us*. The general concurrence, the glorious union of all things, proves the fact.

'Tis not in numbers but in unity that our great strength lies; yet our present numbers are sufficient to repel the force of all the world. The continent has at this time the largest body of armed and disciplined men of any power under heaven: and is just arrived at that pitch of strength, in which no single colony is able to support itself, and the whole, when united, is able to do any thing. Our land force is more than sufficient, and as to naval affairs, we cannot be insensible that Britain would never suffer an American man of war to be built, while the continent remained in her hands. Wherefore, we should be no forwarder a hundred years hence in that branch than we are now; but the truth is, we should be less so, because the timber of the country is every day diminishing, and that which will remain at last, will be far off or difficult to procure.

Were the continent crowded with inhabitants, her sufferings under the present circumstances would be intolerable. The more seaport-towns we had, the more should we have both to defend and to lose. Our present numbers are so happily proportioned to our wants, that no man need be idle. The diminution of trade affords an army, and the necessities of an army create a new trade.

Debts we have none : and whatever we may contract on this account will serve as a glorious memento of our virtue. Can we but leave posterity with a settled form of government, an independent constitution of its own, the purchase at any price will be cheap. But to expend millions for the sake of getting a few vile acts repealed, and routing the present ministry only, is unworthy the charge, and is using posterity with the utmost cruelty ; because it is leaving them the great work to do, and a debt upon their backs from which they derive no advantage. Such a thought's unworthy a man of honor, and is the true characteristic of a narrow heart and a pidling politician.

The debt we may contract doth not deserve our regard if the work be but accomplished. No nation ought to be without a debt. A national debt is a national bond ; and when it bears no interest, is in no case a grievance. Britain is oppressed with a debt of upwards of one hundred and forty millions sterling, for which she pays upwards of four millions interest. And as a compensation for her debt, she has a large navy. America is without a debt, and without a navy ; yet for the twentieth part of the English national debt, could have a navy as large again.

The infant state of the colonies, as it is called, so far from being against, is an argument in favor of independence. We are sufficiently numerous, and were

we more so we might be less united. 'Tis a matter
worthy of observation, that the more a country is
peopled, the smaller their armies are. In military numbers, the ancients far exceeded the moderns : and the
reason is evident, for trade being the consequence of
population, men became too much absorbed thereby to
attend to any thing else. Commerce diminishes the
spirit both of patriotism and military defence. And
history sufficiently informs us, that the bravest achieve-
ments were always accomplished in the non-age of a
nation. With the increase of commerce England hath
lost its spirit. The city of London, notwithstanding
its numbers, submits to continued insults with the
patience of a coward. The more men have to lose,
the less willing are they to venture. The rich are
in general slaves to fear, and submit to courtly power
with the trembling duplicity of a spaniel.

Youth is the seed-time of good habits as well in
nations as in individuals. It might be difficult, if not
impossible, to form the continent into one government
half a century hence. The vast variety of interests,
occasioned by an increase of trade and population,
would create confusion. Colony would be against
colony. Each being able would scorn each other's
assistance : and while the proud and foolish gloried
in their little distinctions, the wise would lament that
the union had not been formed before. Wherefore
the present time is the true time for establishing it.
The intimacy which is contracted in infancy, and the
friendship which is formed in misfortune, are of all
others the most lasting and unalterable. Our present
union is marked with both these characters : we are
young, and we have been distressed ; but our concord
hath withstood our troubles, and fixes a memorable
era for posterity to glory in.

The present time, likewise, is that peculiar time
which never happens to a nation but once, viz. the

time of forming itself into a government. Most nations have let slip the opportunity, and by that means have been compelled to receive laws from their conquerors, instead of making laws for themselves. First, they had a king, and then a form of government ; whereas the articles or charter of government should be formed first, and men delegated to execute them afterwards : but from the errors of other nations let us learn wisdom, and lay hold of the present opportunity — *to begin government at the right end.*

When William the Conqueror subdued England, he gave them law at the point of the sword ; and, until we consent that the seat of government in America be legally and authoritatively occupied, we shall be in danger of having it filled by some fortunate ruffian, who may treat us in the same manner, and then, where will be our freedom ? where our property ?

On a previous page I threw out a few thoughts on the propriety of a Continental Charter (for I only presume to offer hints, not plans) and in this place, I take the liberty of re-mentioning the subject, by observing, that a charter is to be understood as a bond of solemn obligation, which the whole enters into, to support the right of every separate part, whether of religion, professional freedom, or property. A firm bargain and a right reckoning make long friends.

I have heretofore likewise mentioned the necessity of a large and equal representation ; and there is no political matter which more deserves our attention. A small number of electors, or a small number of representatives, are equally dangerous. But if the number of the representatives be not only small, but unequal, the danger is encreased.

Immediate necessity makes many things convenient, which if continued would grow into oppressions. Expedience and right are different things. When the calamities of America required a consultation, there was no method so ready, or at that time so proper, as to appoint persons from the several houses of Assembly for that purpose; and the wisdom with which they have proceeded hath preserved this continent from ruin. But as it is more than probable that we shall never be without a CONGRESS, every well wisher to good order must own that the mode for choosing members of that body, deserves consideration. And I put it as a question to those who make a study of mankind, whether representation and election is not too great a power for one and the same body of men to possess? When we are planning for posterity, we ought to remember that virtue is not hereditary.

To CONCLUDE, however strange it may appear to some, or however unwilling they may be to think so, matters not, but many strong and striking reasons may be given to show, that nothing can settle our affairs so expeditiously as an open and determined DECLARATION FOR INDEPENDENCE. Some of which are,

First — It is the custom of nations, when any two are at war, for some other powers, not engaged in the quarrel, to step in as mediators, and bring about the preliminaries of a peace: But while America calls herself the subject of Great Britain, no power, however well disposed she may be, can offer her mediation. Wherefore, in our present state we may quarrel on for ever.

Secondly — It is unreasonable to suppose, that France or Spain will give us any kind of assistance, if we mean only to make use of that assistance for the purpose of repairing the breach, and strengthening the connection between Britain and America; because, those powers would be sufferers by the consequences.

Thirdly — While we profess ourselves the subjects of Britain, we must, in the eyes of foreign nations, be considered as Rebels. The precedent is somewhat dangerous to their peace, for men to be in arms under the name of subjects : we, on the spot, can solve the paradox ; but to unite resistance and subjection, requires an idea much too refined for common understanding.

Fourthly — Were a manifesto to be published, and despatched to foreign courts, setting forth the miseries we have endured, and the peaceful methods which we have ineffectually used for redress ; declaring at the same time, that not being able any longer to live happily or safely under the cruel disposition of the British court, we had been driven to the necessity of breaking off all connections with her ; at the same time, assuring all such courts of our peaceable disposition towards them, and of our desire of entering into trade with them : such a memorial would produce more good effects to this continent, than if a ship were freighted with petitions to Britain.

Under our present denomination of British subjects, we can neither be received nor heard abroad : the custom of all courts is against us, and will be so, until by an independence we take rank with other nations.

These proceedings may at first seem strange and difficult, but like all other steps which we have already passed over, will in a little time become familiar and agreeable : and until an independence is declared, the continent will feel itself like a man who continues putting off some unpleasant business from day to day, yet knows it must be done, hates to set about it, wishes it over, and is continually haunted with the thoughts of its necessity.

APPENDIX TO "COMMON SENSE"

Since the publication of the first edition of this pamphlet, or rather, on the same day on which it came out, the king's speech made its appearance in this city [Philadelphia]. Had the spirit of prophecy directed the birth of this production, it could not have brought it forth at a more seasonable juncture, or at a more necessary time. The bloody-mindedness of the one, shows the necessity of pursuing the doctrine of the other. Men read by way of revenge. And the speech, instead of terrifying, prepared a way for the manly principles of independence.

Ceremony, and even silence, from whatever motives they may arise, have a hurtful tendency when they give the least degree of countenance to base and wicked performances; wherefore, if this maxim be admitted, it naturally follows, that the king's speech, as being a piece of finished villainy, deserved and still deserves, a general execration, both by the Congress and the people. Yet, as the domestic tranquillity of a nation, depends greatly on the *chastity* of what might properly be called NATIONAL MANNERS, it is often better to pass some things over in silent disdain, than to make use of such new methods of dislike, as might introduce the least innovation on that guardian of our peace and safety. And, perhaps, it is chiefly owing to this prudent delicacy, that the king's speech hath not before now suffered a public execution. The speech, if it may be called one, is nothing better than a wilful audacious libel against the truth, the common good, and the existence of mankind; and is a formal and pompous method of offering up human sacrifices to the pride of tyrants. But this general massacre of mankind, is one of the privileges and the certain consequences of kings; for as nature knows them *not*, they know *not her*, and although they are beings of our *own* creating, they know not *us*, and are become the gods of their creators. The speech hath one good quality, which is, that it is not calculated to deceive, neither can we, even if we would, be deceived by it. Brutality and tyranny appear on the face of it. It leaves us at no loss: And every line convinces, even in the moment of reading, that he who hunts the woods for prey, the naked and untutored Indian, is less savage than the king of Britain.

However, it matters very little now what the king of England either says or does ; he hath wickedly broken through every moral and human obligation, trampled nature and conscience beneath his feet, and by a steady and constitutional spirit of insolence and cruelty procured for himself an universal hatred. It is *now* the interest of America to provide for herself.

The present state of America is truly alarming to every man who is capable of reflection. Without law, without government, without any other mode of power than what is founded on, and granted by, courtesy. Held together by an unexampled occurrence of sentiment, which is nevertheless subject to change, and which every secret enemy is endeavoring to dissolve. Our present condition is, Legislation without law ; wisdom without a plan ; a constitution without a name ; and, what is strangely astonishing, perfect independence contending for dependence. The instance is without a precedent, the case never existed before, and who can tell what may be the event ? The property of no man is secure in the present unbraced system of things. The mind of the multitude is left at random, and seeing no fixed object before them, they pursue such as fancy or opinion presents. Nothing is criminal ; there is no such thing as treason ; wherefore, every one thinks himself at liberty to act as he pleases. The Tories would not have dared to assemble offensively, had they known that their lives, by that act, were forfeited to the laws of the state. A line of distinction should be drawn between English soldiers taken in battle, and inhabitants of America taken in arms. The first are prisoners, but the latter traitors. The one forfeits his liberty, the other his head.

Notwithstanding our wisdom, there is a visible feebleness in some of our proceedings which gives encouragement to dissensions. The continental belt is too loosely buckled : And if something is not done in time, it will be too late to do any thing, and we shall fall into a state, in which neither reconciliation nor independence will be practicable. The king and his worthless adherents are got at their old game of dividing the continent, and there are not wanting among us printers who will be busy in spreading specious falsehoods. The artful and hypocritical letter which appeared a few months ago in two of the New York papers, and likewise in two others, is an evidence that there are men who want both judgment and honesty.

It is easy getting into holes and corners, and talking of reconciliation : But do such men seriously consider how difficult the task is, and how dangerous it may prove, should the continent divide thereon ? Do they take within their view all the various orders of men whose situation and circumstances, as well as their own, are to be considered therein ? Do they put themselves in the place of the sufferer whose *all* is *already* gone, and of the soldier, who hath quitted *all* for the defence of his country ? If their ill-judged moderation be suited to their own private situations *only*, regardless of others, the event will convince them that "they are reckoning without their host."

Put us, say some, on the footing we were in the year 1763 : To which I answer, the request is not now in the power of Britain to comply with, neither will she propose it ; but if it were, and even should be granted, I ask, as a reasonable question, By what means is such a corrupt and faithless court to be kept to its engagements ? Another parliament, nay, even the present, may hereafter repeal the obligation, on the pretence of its being violently obtained, or unwisely granted ; and, in that case, Where is our redress ? No going to law with nations ; cannon are the barristers of crowns ;

and the sword, not of justice, but of war, decides the suit. To be on the footing of 1763, it is not sufficient, that the laws only be put in the same state, but, that our circumstances likewise be put in the same state; our burnt and destroyed towns repaired or built up, our private losses made good, our public debts (contracted for defence) discharged; otherwise we shall be millions worse than we were at that enviable period. Such a request, had it been complied with a year ago, would have won the heart and soul of the continent, but now it is too late. "The Rubicon is passed."

Besides, the taking up arms, merely to enforce the repeal of a pecuniary law, seems as unwarrantable by the divine law, and as repugnant to human feelings, as the taking up arms to enforce obedience thereto. The object, on either side, doth not justify the means; for the lives of men are too valuable to be cast away on such trifles. It is the violence which is done and threatened to our persons; the destruction of our property by an armed force; the invasion of our country by fire and sword, which conscientiously qualifies the use of arms: and the instant in which such mode of defence became necessary, all subjection to Britain ought to have ceased; and the independence of America should have been considered as dating its era from, and published by, *the first musket that was fired against her*. This line is a line of consistency; neither drawn by caprice, nor extended by ambition; but produced by a chain of events, of which the colonies were not the authors.

I shall conclude these remarks, with the following timely and well-intended hints. We ought to reflect, that there are three different ways by which an independency may hereafter be effected; and that *one* of those *three*, will, one day or other, be the fate of America, viz. By the legal voice of the people in Congress; by a military power; or by a mob: It may not always happen that our soldiers are citizens, and the multitude

a body of reasonable men ; virtue, as I have already remarked, is not hereditary, neither is it perpetual. Should
an independency be brought about by the first of those
means, we have every opportunity and every encouragement before us, to form the noblest, purest constitution
on the face of the earth. We have it in our power to
begin the world over again. A situation, similar to the
present, hath not happened since the days of Noah until
now. The birthday of a new world is at hand, and a
race of men, perhaps as numerous as all Europe contains,
are to receive their portion of freedom from the events
of a few months. The reflection is awful, and in this
point of view, how trifling, how ridiculous, do the little
paltry cavilings of a few weak or interested men appear, when weighed against the business of a world.

Should we neglect the present favorable and inviting
period, and independence be hereafter effected by any
other means, we must charge the consequence to ourselves, or to those rather whose narrow and prejudiced
souls are habitually opposing the measure, without either
inquiring or reflecting. There are reasons to be given
in support of independence which men should rather
privately think of, than be publicly told of. We ought
not now to be debating whether we shall be independent
or not, but anxious to accomplish it on a firm, secure,
and honorable basis, and uneasy rather that it is not yet
began upon. Every day convinces us of its necessity.
Even the Tories (if such beings yet remain among us)
should, of all men, be the most solicitous to promote it ;
for as the appointment of committees at first protected
them from popular rage, so, a wise and well established
form of government will be the only certain means of
continuing it securely to them. Wherefore, if they
have not virtue enough to be WHIGS, they ought to
have prudence enough to wish for independence.

In short, independence is the only bond that tie and
keep us together. We shall then see our object, and

our ears will be legally shut against the schemes of an intriguing, as well as cruel, enemy. We shall then, too, be on a proper footing to treat with Britain ; for there is reason to conclude, that the pride of that court will be less hurt by treating with the American States for terms of peace, than with those, whom she denominates "rebellious subjects," for terms of accommodation. It is our delaying in that, encourages her to hope for conquest, and our backwardness tends only to prolong the war. As we have, without any good effect therefrom, withheld our trade to obtain a redress of our grievances, let us now try the alternative, by independently redressing them ourselves, and then offering to open the trade. The mercantile and reasonable part of England, will be still with us ; because, peace, with trade, is preferable to war without it. And if this offer be not accepted, other courts may be applied to.

On these grounds I rest the matter. And as no offer hath yet been made to refute the doctrine contained in the former editions of this pamphlet, it is a negative proof, that either the doctrine cannot be refuted, or, that the party in favor of it are too numerous to be opposed. WHEREFORE, instead of gazing at each other with suspicious or doubtful curiosity, let each of us hold out to his neighbor the hearty hand of friendship, and unite in drawing a line, which, like an act of oblivion, shall bury in forgetfulness every former dissension. Let the names of Whig and Tory be extinct ; and let none other be heard among us, than those of *a good citizen* ; *an open and resolute friend* ; and *a virtuous supporter of the* RIGHTS *of* MANKIND, *and of the* FREE AND INDEPENDENT STATES OF AMERICA.

THE AMERICAN CRISIS

These are the times that try men's souls. The summer soldier and the sunshine patriot will, in this crisis, shrink from the service of their country ; but he that stands it *now*, deserves the love and thanks of man and woman. Tyranny, like hell, is not easily conquered ; yet we have this consolation with us, that the harder the conflict, the more glorious the triumph. What we obtain too cheap, we esteem too lightly : it is dearness only that gives every thing its value. Heaven knows how to put a proper price upon its goods ; and it would be strange indeed if so celestial an article as FREEDOM should not be highly rated. Britain, with an army to enforce her tyranny, has declared that she has a right (*not only to* TAX) but "to BIND *us in* ALL CASES WHATSOEVER," and if being *bound in that manner*, is not slavery, then is there not such a thing as slavery upon earth. Even the expression is impious ; for so unlimited a power can belong only to God.

Whether the independence of the continent was declared too soon, or delayed too long, I will not now enter into as an argument ; my own simple opinion is, that had it been eight months earlier, it would have been much better. We did not make a proper use of last winter, neither could we, while we were in a dependent state. However, the fault, if it were one, was all our own ; we have none to blame but ourselves. But no great deal is lost yet. All that Howe has been doing for this month past, is rather a ravage than a conquest, which the spirit of the Jerseys, a year ago, would have quickly repulsed, and which time and a little resolution will soon recover.

I have as little superstition in me as any man living, but my secret opinion has ever been, and still is, that

God Almighty will not give up a people to military destruction, or leave them unsupportedly to perish, who have so earnestly and so repeatedly sought to avoid the calamities of war, by every decent method which wisdom could invent. Neither have I so much of the infidel in me, as to suppose that He has relinquished the government of the world, and given us up to the care of devils ; and as I do not, I cannot see on what grounds the king of Britain can look up to heaven for help against us : a common murderer, a highwayman, or a house-breaker, has as good a pretence as he.

'Tis surprising to see how rapidly a panic will sometimes run through a country. All nations and ages have been subject to them. Britain has trembled like an ague at the report of a French fleet of flat-bottomed boats ; and in the fifteenth century the whole English army, after ravaging the kingdom of France, was driven back like men petrified with fear ; and this brave exploit was performed by a few broken forces collected and headed by a woman, Joan of Arc. Would that heaven might inspire some Jersey maid to spirit up her countrymen, and save her fair fellow sufferers from ravage and ravishment ! Yet panics, in some cases, have their uses ; they produce as much good as hurt. Their duration is always short ; the mind soon grows through them, and acquires a firmer habit than before. But their peculiar advantage is, that they are the touchstones of sincerity and hypocrisy, and bring things and men to light, which might otherwise have lain for ever undiscovered. In fact, they have the same effect on secret traitors, which an imaginary apparition would have upon a private murderer. They sift out the hidden thoughts of man, and hold them up in public to the world. Many a disguised Tory has lately shown his head, that shall penitentially solemnize with curses the day on which Howe arrived upon the Delaware.

As I was with the troops at Fort Lee, and marched
with them to the edge of Pennsylvania, I am well acquainted with many circumstances, which those who
live at a distance know but little or nothing of.   Our situation there was exceedingly cramped, the place being a
narrow neck of land between the North River and the
Hackensack.   Our force was inconsiderable, being not
one-fourth so great as Howe could bring against us.
We had no army at hand to have relieved the garrison,
had we shut ourselves up and stood on our defence.
Our ammunition, light artillery, and the best part of
our stores, had been removed, on the apprehension that
Howe would endeavor to penetrate the Jerseys, in
which case Fort Lee could be of no use to us; for it
must occur to every thinking man, whether in the army
or not, that these kind of field forts are only for temporary purposes, and last in use no longer than the enemy
directs his force against the particular object which
such forts are raised to defend.   Such was our situation
and condition at Fort Lee on the morning of the 20th
of November, when an officer arrived with information that the enemy with 200 boats had landed about
seven miles above; Major General Nathaniel Green,
who commanded the garrison, immediately ordered
them under arms, and sent express to General Washington at the town of Hackensack, distant by the way
of the ferry = six miles.   Our first object was to secure
the bridge over the Hackensack, which laid up the
river between the enemy and us, about six miles from
us, and three from them.   General Washington arrived in about three-quarters of an hour, and marched
at the head of the troops towards the bridge, which
place I expected we should have a brush for; however, they did not choose to dispute it with us, and the
greatest part of our troops went over the bridge, the
rest over the ferry, except some which passed at a mill

on a small creek, between the bridge and the ferry, and made their way through some marshy grounds up to the town of Hackensack, and there passed the river. We brought off as much baggage as the wagons could contain, the rest was lost. The simple object was to bring off the garrison, and march them on till they could be strengthened by the Jersey or Pennsylvania militia, so as to be enabled to make a stand. We staid four days at Newark, collected our out-posts with some of the Jersey militia, and marched out twice to meet the enemy, on being informed that they were advancing, though our numbers were greatly inferior to theirs. Howe, in my little opinion, committed a great error in generalship in not throwing a body of forces off from Staten Island through Amboy, by which means he might have seized all our stores at Brunswick, and intercepted our march into Pennsylvania ; but if we believe the power of hell to be limited, we must likewise believe that their agents are under some providential control.

I shall not now attempt to give all the particulars of our retreat to the Delaware ; suffice it for the present to say, that both officers and men, though greatly harassed and fatigued, frequently without rest, covering, or provision, the inevitable consequences of a long retreat, bore it with a manly and martial spirit. All their wishes centred in one, which was, that the country would turn out and help them to drive the enemy back. Voltaire has remarked that King William never appeared to full advantage but in difficulties and in action ; the same remark may be made on General Washington, for the character fits him. There is a natural firmness in some minds which cannot be unlocked by trifles, but which, when unlocked, discovers a cabinet of fortitude ; and I reckon it among those kind of public blessings, which we do not immediately see, that God hath blessed him with uninterrupted health, and given him a mind that can even flourish upon care.

I love the man that can smile in trouble, that can gather strength from distress, and grow brave by reflection. 'Tis the business of little minds to shrink ; but he whose heart is firm, and whose conscience approves his conduct, will pursue his principles unto death. My own line of reasoning is to myself as straight and clear as a ray of light. Not all the treasures of the world, so far as I believe, could have induced me to support an offensive war, for I think it murder ; but if a thief breaks into my house, burns and destroys my property, and kills or threatens to kill me, or those that are in it, and to *"bind me in all cases whatsoever"* to his absolute will, am I to suffer it ? What signifies it to me, whether he who does it is a king or a common man ; my countryman or not my countryman ; whether it be done by an individual villain, or an army of them ? If we reason to the root of things we shall find no difference ; neither can any just cause be assigned why we should punish in the one case and pardon in the other. Let them call me rebel and welcome, I feel no concern from it ; but I should suffer the misery of devils, were I to make a whore of my soul by swearing allegiance to one whose character is that of a sottish, stupid, stubborn, worthless, brutish man. I conceive likewise a horrid idea in receiving mercy from a being, who at the last day shall be shrieking to the rocks and mountains to cover him, and fleeing with terror from the orphan, the widow, and the slain of America.

There are cases which cannot be overdone by language, and this is one. There are persons, too, who see not the full extent of the evil which threatens them ; they solace themselves with hopes that the enemy, if he succeed, will be merciful. It is the madness of folly, to expect mercy from those who have refused to do justice ; and even mercy, where conquest is the object, is only a trick of war ; the cunning of the fox is as murderous as the violence of the wolf, and we ought to guard equally against both. Howe's first object is, partly by threats and partly by promises, to terrify or seduce the people to deliver up their arms and receive mercy. The ministry recommended the same plan to Gage, and this is what the tories call making their peace, *"a peace which passeth all understanding"* indeed ! A peace which would be the immediate forerunner of a worse ruin than any we have yet thought of. Ye men of Pennsylvania, do reason upon these things ! Were the back counties to give up their arms, they would fall an easy prey to the Indians, who are all armed : this perhaps is what some Tories would not be sorry for. Were the home counties to deliver up their arms, they would be exposed to the resentment of the back counties, who would then have it in their power to chastise their defection at pleasure. And were any one state to give up its arms, *that* state must be garrisoned by all Howe's army of Britons and Hessians to preserve it from the anger of the rest. Mutual fear is the principal link in the chain of mutual love, and woe be to that state that breaks the compact. Howe is mercifully inviting you to barbarous destruction, and men must be either rogues or fools that will not see it. I dwell not upon the vapors of imagination ; I bring reason to your ears, and, in language as plain as A, B, C, hold up truth to your eyes.

I thank God, that I fear not. I see no real cause for fear. I know our situation well, and can see the way out of it. While our army was collected, Howe dared not risk a battle ; and it is no credit to him that he decamped from the White Plains, and waited a mean opportunity to ravage the defenceless Jerseys ; but it is great credit to us, that, with a handful of men, we sustained an orderly retreat for near an hundred miles, brought off our ammunition, all our field pieces, the greatest part of our stores, and had four rivers to pass. None can say that our retreat was precipitate, for we were near three weeks in performing it, that the country might have time to come in. Twice we marched back to meet the enemy, and remained out till dark. The sign of fear was not seen in our camp, and had not some of the cowardly and disaffected inhabitants spread false alarms through the country, the Jerseys had never been ravaged. Once more we are again collected and collecting ; our new army at both ends of the continent is recruiting fast, and we shall be able to open the next campaign with sixty thousand men, well armed and clothed. This is our situation, and who will may know it. By perseverance and fortitude we have the prospect of a glorious issue ; by cowardice and submission, the sad choice of a variety of evils — a ravaged country — a depopulated city — habitations without safety, and slavery without hope — our homes turned into barracks and bawdy-houses for Hessians, and a future race to provide for, whose fathers we shall doubt of. Look on this picture and weep over it ! and if there yet remains one thoughtless wretch who believes it not, let him suffer it unlamented.

COMMON SENSE

December 23, 1776

To Lord Howe

"What's in the name of *lord*, that I should fear
To bring my grievance to the public ear ?"

CHURCHILL

Universal empire is the prerogative of a writer. His concerns are with all mankind, and though he cannot command their obedience, he can assign them their duty. The Republic of Letters is more ancient than monarchy, and of far higher character in the world than the vassal court of Britain ; he that rebels against reason is a real rebel, but he that in defence of reason rebels against tyranny has a better title to *"Defender of the Faith,"* than George the Third.

As a military man your lordship may hold out the sword of war, and call it the *"ultima ratio regum"* : *the last reason of kings* ; we in return can show you the sword of justice, and call it "the best scourge of tyrants." The first of these two may threaten, or even frighten for a while, and cast a sickly languor over an insulted people, but reason will soon recover the debauch, and restore them again to tranquil fortitude. Your lordship, I find, has now commenced author, and published a proclamation ; I have published a *Crisis*. As they stand, they are the antipodes of each other ; both cannot rise at once, and one of them must descend ; and so quick is the revolution of things, that your lordship's performance, I see, has already fallen many degrees from its first place, and is now just visible on the edge of the political horizon.

It is surprising to what a pitch of infatuation, blind folly and obstinacy will carry mankind, and your lordship's drowsy proclamation is a proof that it does not even quit them in their sleep. Perhaps you thought America too was taking a nap, and therefore chose, like Satan to Eve, to whisper the delusion softly, lest you should awaken her. This continent, sir, is too extensive to sleep all at once, and too watchful, even in its slumbers, not to startle at the unhallowed foot of an invader. You may issue your proclamations, and welcome, for we have learned to "reverence overselves," and scorn the insulting ruffian that employs you. America, for your deceased brother's sake, would gladly have shown you respect and it is a new aggravation to her feelings, that Howe should be forgetful, and raise his sword against those, who at their own charge raised a monument to his brother.* But your master has commanded, and you have not enough of nature left to

* George Augustus Howe.

refuse. Surely there must be something strangely degenerating in the love of monarchy, that can so completely wear a man down to an ingrate, and make him proud to lick the dust that kings have trod upon. A few more years, should you survive them, will bestow on you the title of "an old man" : and in some hour of future reflection you may probably find the fitness of Wolsey's despairing penitence — "had I served my God as faithfully as I have served my king, he would not thus have forsaken me in my old age."

The character you appear to us in, is truly ridiculous. Your friends, the Tories, announced your coming, with high descriptions of your unlimited powers ; but your proclamation has given them the lie, by showing you to be a commissioner without authority. Had your powers been ever so great they were nothing to us, further than we pleased ; because we had the same right which other nations had, to do what we thought was best. "*The* UNITED STATES *of* AMERICA," will sound as pompously in the world or in history, as "the kingdom of Great Britain" ; the character of *General Washington* will fill a page with as much lustre as that of *Lord Howe* : and the *Congress* have as much right to command the *king and Parliament* in London to desist from legislation, as *they* or *you* have to command the Congress. Only suppose how laughable such an edict would appear from us, and then, in that merry mood, do but turn the tables upon yourself, and you will see how your proclamation is received here. Having thus placed you in a proper position in which you may have a full view of your folly, and learn to despise it, I hold up to you, for that purpose, the following quotation from your own lunarian proclamation. — "And we (Lord Howe and General Howe) do command (and in his majesty's name forsooth) all such persons as are assembled together, under the name of general or provincial congresses, committees, conventions or other associations, by whatever name or names known and distinguished, to desist and cease from all such treasonable actings and doings."

Why, God bless me ! what have you to do with our independence ? We ask no leave of yours to set it up ; we ask no money of yours to support it ; we can do better without your fleets and armies than with them ; you may soon have enough to do to protect yourselves without being burdened with us. We are very willing to be at peace with you, to buy of you and sell to you, and, like young beginners in the world, to work for our living ; therefore, why do you put yourselves out of cash, when we know you cannot spare it, and we do not desire you to run into debt ?

Had you gained an entire conquest over all the armies of America, and then put forth a proclamation, offering (what you call) mercy, your conduct would have had some specious show of humanity ; but to creep by surprise into a province, and there endeavor to terrify and seduce the inhabitants from their just allegiance to the rest by promises, which you neither meant nor were able to fulfil, is both cruel and unmanly : cruel in its effects ; because, unless you can keep all the ground you have marched over, how are you, in the words of your proclamation, to secure to your proselytes "the enjoyment of their property" ? What is to become either of your new adopted subjects, or your old friends, the Tories, in Burlington, Bordentown, Trenton, Mount Holly, and many other places, where you proudly lorded it for a few days, and then fled with the precipitation of a pursued thief ? What, I say, is to become of those wretches ? What is to become of those who went over to you from this city and State ? What more can you say to them than "shift for yourselves" ? Or what more can they hope for than to wander like vagabonds over the face of the earth ? You may now tell them to take their leave of America, and all that once was theirs. Recommend them, for consolation, to your master's court ; there perhaps they may make a shift to live on the scraps of some dangling parasite, and choose companions among thousands like themselves. A traitor is the foulest fiend on earth.

In a political sense we ought to thank you for thus bequeathing estates to the continent ; we shall soon, at this rate, be able to carry on a war without expense, and grow rich by the ill policy of Lord Howe, and the generous defection of the Tories. Had you set your foot into this city, you would have bestowed estates upon us which we never thought of, by bringing forth traitors we were unwilling to suspect. But these men, you'll say, "are his majesty's most faithful subjects" ; let that honor, then, be all their fortune, and let his majesty take them to himself.

I am now thoroughly disgusted with them ; they live in ungrateful ease, and bend their whole minds to mischief. It seems as if God had given them over to a spirit of infidelity, and that they are open to conviction in no other line but that of punishment. It is time to have done with tarring, feathering, carting, and taking securities for their future good behavior ; every sensible man must feel a conscious shame at seeing a poor fellow hawked for a show about the streets, when it is known he is only the tool of some principal villain, biassed into his offence by the force of false reasoning, or bribed thereto, through sad necessity. We dishonor ourselves by attacking such trifling characters while greater ones are suffered to escape ; 'tis our duty to find *them* out, and their proper punishment would be to exile them from the continent for ever. The circle of them is not so great as some imagine ; the influence of a few have tainted many who are not naturally corrupt. A continual circulation of lies among those who are not much in the way of hearing them contradicted, will in time pass for truth ; and the crime lies not in the believer but the inventor. I am not for declaring war with every man that appears not so warm as myself : difference of constitution, temper, habit of speaking, and many other things, will go a great way in fixing the outward character of a man, yet simple honesty may remain at bottom. Some men have naturally a military turn, and can brave hardships and the risk of life with a cheerful face ; others have not ; no slavery appears to them so great as the fatigue of arms, and no terror so powerful as that of personal danger. What can we say ? We cannot alter nature, neither ought we to punish the son because the father begot him in a cowardly mood. However, I believe most men have more courage than they know of, and that a little at first is enough to begin with. I knew the time when I thought that the whistling of a cannon ball would have frightened me almost to death ; but I have since tried it, and find that I can stand it with as little discomposure, and, I believe, with a much easier conscience than your lordship. The same dread would return to me again were I in your situation, for my solemn belief of your cause is, that it is hellish and damnable, and, under that conviction, every thinking man's heart *must* fail him.

If ever a nation was mad and foolish, blind to its own interest and bent on its own destruction, it is Britain. There are such things as national sins, and though the punishment of individuals may be reserved to *another* world, national punishment can only be inflicted in *this* world. Britain, as a nation, is, in my inmost belief, the greatest and most ungrateful offender against God on the face of the whole earth. Blessed with all the commerce she could wish for, and furnished, by a vast extension of dominion, with the means of civilizing both the eastern and western world, she has made no other use of both than proudly to idolize her own "thunder," and rip up the bowels of whole countries for what she could get. Like Alexander, she has made war her sport, and inflicted misery for prodigality's sake. The blood of India is not yet repaid, nor the wretchedness of Africa yet requited. Of late she has enlarged her list of national cruelties by her butcherly destruction of the Caribbs of St. Vincent's, and returning an answer by the sword to the meek prayer for *"Peace, liberty and safety."* These are serious things, and whatever a foolish tyrant, a debauched court, a trafficking legislature, or a blinded people may think, the national account with heaven must some day or other be settled : all countries have sooner or later been called to their reckoning ; the proudest empires have sunk when the balance was struck ; and Britain, like an individual penitent, must undergo her day of sorrow, and the sooner it happens to her the better. As I wish it over, I wish it to come, but withal wish that it may be as light as possible.

By what means, may I ask, do you expect to conquer America ? If you could not effect it in the summer, when our army was less than yours, nor in the winter, when we had none, how are you to do it ? In point of generalship you have been outwitted, and in point of fortitude outdone ; your advantages turn out to your loss, and show us that it is in our power to ruin you by gifts : like a game of drafts, we can move out of *one* square to let you come in, in order that we may afterwards take two or three for one ; and as we can always keep a double corner for ourselves, we can always prevent a total defeat. You cannot be so insensible as not to see that we have two to one the advantage of you, because we conquer by a drawn game, and you lose by it. Burgoyne might have taught your lordship this knowledge ; he has been long a student in the doctrine of chances.

I have no other idea of conquering countries than by subduing the armies which defend them : have you

done this, or can you do it ?   If you have not, it would
be civil in you to let your proclamations alone for the
present ; otherwise, you will ruin more Tories by your
grace and favor, than you will Whigs by your arms.

Were you to obtain possession of this city, you would
not know what to do with it more than to plunder it.
To hold it in the manner you hold New York, would
be an additional dead weight upon your hands ; and if
a general conquest is your object, you had better be
without the city than with it.   When you have defeated
all our armies, the cities will fall into your hands of
themselves ; but to creep into them in the manner you
got into Princeton, Trenton, &c. is like robbing an
orchard in the night before the fruit be ripe, and running away in the morning.   Your experiment in the
Jerseys is sufficient to teach you that you have something more to do than barely to get into other people's
houses ; and your new converts, to whom you promised
all manner of protection, and seduced into new guilt by
pardoning them from their former virtues, must begin
to have a very contemptible opinion both of your
power and your policy.   Your authority in the Jerseys
is now reduced to the small circle which your army
occupies, and your proclamation is no where else seen
unless it be to be laughed at.   The mighty subduers of
the continent have retreated into a nutshell, and the
proud forgivers of our sins are fled from those they came
to pardon ; and all this at a time when they were des-
patching vessel after vessel to England with the great
news of every day.   In short, you have managed your
Jersey expedition so very dexterously, that the dead
only are conquerors, because none will dispute the
ground with them.

In all the wars which you have formerly been concerned in you had only armies to contend with ; in this
case you have both an army and a country to combat
with.   In former wars, the countries followed the fate

of their capitals ; Canada fell with Quebec, and Minorca
with Port Mahon or St. Phillips ; by subduing those,
the conquerors opened a way into, and became masters
of the country : here it is otherwise ; if you get possession of a city here, you are obliged to shut yourselves
up in it, and can make no other use of it, than to spend
your country's money in.   This is all the advantage
you have drawn from New York ; and you would draw
less from Philadelphia, because it requires more force
to keep it, and is much further from the sea.   A pretty
figure you and the Tories would cut in this city, with
a river full of ice, and a town full of fire ; for the immediate consequence of your getting here would be,
that you would be cannonaded out again, and the Tories
be obliged to make good the damage ; and this sooner
or later will be the fate of New York.

I wish to see the city saved, not so much from military
as from natural motives.   'Tis the hiding place of
women and children, and Lord Howe's proper business
is with our armies.   When I put all the circumstances
together which ought to be taken, I laugh at your
notion of conquering America.   Because you lived in a
little country, where an army might run over the whole
in a few days, and where a single company of soldiers
might put a multitude to the rout, you expected to find
it the same here.   It is plain that you brought over with
you all the narrow notions you were bred up with, and
imagined that a proclamation in the king's name was to
do great things ; but Englishmen always travel for
knowledge, and your lordship, I hope, will return, if
you return at all, much wiser than you came.

We may be surprised by events we did not expect,
and in that interval of recollection you may gain some
temporary advantage : such was the case a few weeks
ago, but we soon ripen again into reason, collect our
strength, and while you are preparing for a triumph,
we come upon you with a defeat.   Such it has been,

and such it would be were you to try it a hundred times over. Were you to garrison the places you might march over, in order to secure their subjection, (for remember you can do it by no other means,) your army would be like a stream of water running to nothing. By the time you extended from New York to Virginia, you would be reduced to a string of drops not capable of hanging together; while we, by retreating from State to State, like a river turning back upon itself, would acquire strength in the same proportion as you lost it, and in the end be capable of overwhelming you. The country, in the meantime, would suffer, but it is a day of suffering, and we ought to expect it. What we contend for is worthy the affliction we may go through. If we get but bread to eat, and any kind of raiment to put on, we ought not only to be contented, but thankful. More than *that* we ought not to look for, and less than *that* heaven has not yet suffered us to want. He that would sell his birthright for a little *salt*, is as worthless as he who sold it for pottage without salt; and he that would part with it for a gay coat, or a plain coat, ought for ever to be a slave in buff. What are salt, sugar and finery, to the inestimable blessings of "Liberty and Safety!" Or what are the inconveniences of a few months to the tributary bondage of ages? The meanest peasant in America, blessed with these sentiments, is a happy man compared with a New York Tory; he can eat his morsel without repining, and when he has done, can sweeten it with a repast of wholesome air; he can take his child by the hand and bless it, without feeling the conscious shame of neglecting a parent's duty.

Suppose our armies in every part of this continent were immediately to disperse, every man to his home, or where else he might be safe, and engage to reassemble again on a certain future day; it is clear that you would then have no army to contend with, yet you would be

as much at a loss in that case as you are now ; you would
be afraid to send your troops in parties over to the
continent, either to disarm or prevent us from assem-
bling, lest they should not return ; and while you kept
them together, having no arms of ours to dispute with,
you could not call it a conquest ; you might furnish
out a pompous page in the London *Gazette* or a New
York paper, but when we returned at the appointed
time, you would have the same work to do that you
had at first.

It has been the folly of Britain to suppose herself more
powerful than she really is, and by that means has ar-
rogated to herself a rank in the world she is not entitled
to : for more than this century past she has not been
able to carry on a war without foreign assistance. In
Marlborough's campaigns, and from that day to this,
the number of German troops and officers assisting her
have been about equal with her own ; ten thousand
Hessians were sent to England last war to protect her
from a French invasion ; and she would have cut but
a poor figure in her Canadian and West Indian expedi-
tions, had not America been lavish both of her money
and men to help her along. The only instance in which
she was engaged singly, that I can recollect, was against
the rebellion in Scotland, in the years 1745 and 1746,
and in that, out of three battles, she was twice beaten, till
by thus reducing their numbers, (as we shall yours) and
taking a supply ship that was coming to Scotland with
clothes, arms and money, (as we have often done,) she
was at last enabled to defeat them. England was never
famous by land ; her officers have generally been sus-
pected of cowardice, have more of the air of a dancing-
master than a soldier, and by the samples which we have
taken prisoners, we give the preference to ourselves.
Her strength, of late, has lain in her extravagance ; but
as her finances and credit are now low, her sinews in that
line begin to fail fast. As a nation she is the poorest in

Europe; for were the whole kingdom, and all that is in it, to be put up for sale like the estate of a bankrupt, it would not fetch as much as she owes; yet this thoughtless wretch must go to war, and with the avowed design, too, of making us beasts of burden, to support her in riot and debauchery, and to assist her afterwards in distressing those nations who are now our best friends.

'Tis the unhappy temper of the English to be pleased with any war, right or wrong, be it but successful; but they soon grow discontented with ill fortune, and it is an even chance that they are as clamorous for peace next summer, as the king and his ministers were for war last winter. In this natural view of things, your lordship stands in a very critical situation: your whole character is now staked upon your laurels; if they wither, you wither with them; if they flourish, you cannot live long to look at them; and at any rate, the black account hereafter is not far off. What lately appeared to us misfortunes, were only blessings in disguise; and the seeming advantages on your side have turned out to our profit. Even our loss of this city, as far as we can see, might be a principal gain to us: the more surface you spread over, the thinner you will be, and the easier wiped away; and our consolation under that apparent disaster would be, that the estates of the Tories would become securities for the repairs. In short, there is no old ground we can fail upon, but some new foundation rises again to support us. "We have put, sir, our hands to the plough, and cursed be he that looketh back."

Your king, in his speech to Parliament last spring, declared, "That he had no doubt but the great force they had enabled him to send to America, would effectually reduce the rebellious colonies." It has not, neither can it; but it has done just enough to lay the foundation of its own next year's ruin. You are sensible that you left England in a divided, distracted state of

politics, and, by the command you had here, you became
a principal prop in the court party ; their fortunes rest
on yours ; by a single express you can fix their value
with the public, and the degree to which their spirits
shall rise or fall ; they are in your hands as stock, and
you have the secret of the *alley* with you. Thus situ-
ated and connected, you become the unintentional
mechanical instrument of your own and their overthrow. The king and his ministers put conquest out
of doubt, and the credit of both depended on the proof.
To support them in the interim, it was necessary that
you should make the most of every thing, and we can
tell by Hugh Gaine's New York paper what the com-
plexion of the London *Gazette* is. With such a list of
victories the nation cannot expect you will ask new
supplies ; and to confess your want of them would give
the lie to your triumphs, and impeach the king and his
ministers of treasonable deception. If you make the
necessary demand at home, your party sinks ; if you
make it not, you sink yourself ; to ask it now is too late,
and to ask it before was too soon, and unless it arrive
quickly will be of no use. In short, the part you have
to act, cannot be acted ; and I am fully persuaded that
all you have to trust to is, to do the best you can with
what force you have got, or little more. Though we
have greatly exceeded you in point of generalship and
bravery of men, yet, as a people, we have not entered
into the full soul of enterprise ; for I, who know England and the disposition of the people well, am con-
fident, that it is easier for us to effect a revolution there,
than you a conquest here ; a few thousand men landed
in England with the declared design of deposing the
present king, bringing his ministers to trial, and setting
up the Duke of Gloucester in his stead, would assuredly
carry their point, while you are grovelling here, ignorant
of the matter. As I send all my papers to England,
this, like *Common Sense*, will find its way there ; and

though it may put one party on their guard, it will inform the other, and the nation in general, of our design to help them.

Thus far, sir, I have endeavored to give you a picture of present affairs : you may draw from it what conclusions you please. I wish as well to the true prosperity of England as you can, but I consider INDEPENDENCE *as America's natural right and interest,* and never could see any real disservice it would be to Britain. If an English merchant receives an order, and is paid for it, it signifies nothing to him who governs the country. This is my creed of politics. If I have any where expressed myself overwarmly, 'tis from a fixed, immovable hatred I have, and ever had, to cruel men and cruel measures. I have likewise an aversion to monarchy, as being too debasing to the dignity of man ; but I never troubled others with my notions till very lately, nor ever published a syllable in England in my life. What I write is pure nature, and my pen and my soul have ever gone together. My writings I have always given away, reserving only the expence of printing and paper, and sometimes not even that. I never courted either fame or interest, and my manner of life, to those who know it, will justify what I say. My study is to be useful, and if your lordship loves mankind as well as I do, you would, seeing you cannot conquer us, cast about and lend your hand towards accomplishing a peace. Our independence with God's blessing we will maintain against all the world ; but as we wish to avoid evil ourselves, we wish not to inflict it on others. I am never over-inquisitive into the secrets of the cabinet, but I have some notion that, if you neglect the present opportunity, it will not be in our power to make a separate peace with you afterwards ; for whatever treaties or alliances we form, we shall most faithfully abide by ; wherefore you may be deceived if you think you can make it with us at any time. A lasting independent peace is my wish, end and aim ; and to accomplish that, *"I pray God the* Americans *may never be defeated, and I trust while they have good officers, and are well commanded,"* and willing to be commanded, *"that they* NEVER WILL BE."

COMMON SENSE

PHILADELPHIA, Jan. 13, 1777

THOUGHTS ON THE PEACE, AND THE PROBABLE ADVANTAGES THEREOF

"The times that tried men's souls," are over — and the greatest and completest revolution the world ever knew, gloriously and happily accomplished.

But to pass from the extremes of danger to safety — from the tumult of war to the tranquillity of peace, though sweet in contemplation, requires a gradual composure of the senses to receive it. Even calmness has the power of stunning, when it opens too instantly upon us. The long and raging hurricane that should cease in a moment, would leave us in a state rather of wonder than enjoyment ; and some moments of recollection must pass, before we could be capable of tasting the felicity of repose. There are but few instances, in which the mind is fitted for sudden transitions : it takes in its pleasures by reflection and comparison and those must have time to act, before the relish for new scenes is complete.

In the present case — the mighty magnitude of the object — the various uncertainties of fate it has undergone — the numerous and complicated dangers we have suffered or escaped — the eminence we now stand on, and the vast prospect before us, must all conspire to impress us with contemplation.

To see it in our power to make a world happy — to teach mankind the art of being so — to exhibit, on the

theatre of the universe a character hitherto unknown —
and to have, as it were, a new creation intrusted to our
hands, are honors that command reflection, and can neither be too highly estimated, nor too gratefully received.

In this pause then of recollection — while the storm
is ceasing, and the long agitated mind vibrating to a rest,
let us look back on the scenes we have passed, and learn
from experience what is yet to be done.

Never, I say, had a country so many openings to happiness as this. Her setting out in life, like the rising of
a fair morning, was unclouded and promising. Her
cause was good. Her principles just and liberal. Her
temper serene and firm. Her conduct regulated by
the nicest steps, and everything about her wore the
mark of honor. It is not every country (perhaps there
is not another in the world) that can boast so fair an
origin. Even the first settlement of America corre-
sponds with the character of the revolution. Rome,
once the proud mistress of the universe, was originally
a band of ruffians. Plunder and rapine made her rich,
and her oppression of millions made her great. But
America need never be ashamed to tell her birth, nor
relate the stages by which she rose to empire.

The remembrance, then, of what is past, if it operates
rightly, must inspire her with the most laudable of all
ambition, that of adding to the fair fame she began with.
The world has seen her great in adversity ; struggling,
without a thought of yielding, beneath accumulated
difficulties, bravely, nay proudly, encountering distress,
and rising in resolution as the storm increased. All this
is justly due to her, for her fortitude has merited the
character. Let, then, the world see that she can bear
prosperity : and that her honest virtue in time of peace,
is equal to the bravest virtue in time of war.

She is now descending to the scenes of quiet and

domestic life. Not beneath the cypress shade of disappointment, but to enjoy in her own land, and under
her own vine, the sweet of her labors, and the reward
of her toil. — In this situation, may she never forget
that a fair national reputation is of as much importance
as independence. That it possesses a charm that wins
upon the world, and makes even enemies civil. That
it gives a dignity which is often superior to power, and
commands reverence where pomp and splendor fail.

It would be a circumstance ever to be lamented and
never to be forgotten, were a single blot, from any cause
whatever, suffered to fall on a revolution, which to the
end of time must be an honor to the age that accomplished it : and which has contributed more to en-
lighten the world, and diffuse a spirit of freedom and
liberality among mankind, than any human event (if this
may be called one) that ever preceded it.

It is not among the least of the calamities of a long
continued war, that it unhinges the mind from those
nice sensations which at other times appear so amiable.
The continual spectacle of woe blunts the finer feelings,
and the necessity of bearing with the sight, renders it
familiar. In like manner, are many of the moral obligations of society weakened, till the custom of acting by
necessity becomes an apology, where it is truly a crime.
Yet let but a nation conceive rightly of its character,
and it will be chastely just in protecting it. None ever
began with a fairer than America and none can be under
a greater obligation to preserve it.

The debt which America has contracted, compared
with the cause she has gained, and the advantages to
flow from it, ought scarcely to be mentioned. She has
it in her choice to do, and to live as happily as she pleases.
The world is in her hands. She has no foreign power
to monopolize her commerce, perplex her legislation,
or control her prosperity. The struggle is over, which

must one day have happened, and, perhaps, never could have happened at a better time.* And instead of a domineering master, she has gained an *ally* whose exemplary greatness, and universal liberality, have extorted a confession even from her enemies.

With the blessings of peace, independence, and an universal commerce, the states, individually and collectively, will have leisure and opportunity to regulate and establish their domestic concerns, and to put it beyond the power of calumny to throw the least reflection on their honor. Character is much easier kept than recovered, and that man, if any such there be, who, from sinister views, or littleness of soul, lends unseen his hand to injure it, contrives a wound it will never be in his power to heal.

As we have established an inheritance for posterity, let

---

* That the revolution began at the exact period of time best fitted to the purpose, is sufficiently proved by the event. – But the great hinge on which the whole machine turned, is the *Union of the States :* and this union was naturally produced by the inability of any one state to support itself against any foreign enemy without the assistance of the rest.

Had the states severally been less able than they were when the war began, their united strength would not have been equal to the undertaking, and they must in all human probability have failed. – And, on the other hand, had they severally been more able, they might not have seen, or, what is more, might not have felt, the necessity of uniting : and, either by attempting to stand alone or in small confederacies, would have been separately conquered.

Now, as we cannot see a time (and many years must pass away before it can arrive) when the strength of any one state, or several united, can be equal to the whole of the present United States, and as we have seen the extreme difficulty of collectively prosecuting the war to a successful issue, and preserving our national importance in the world, therefore, from the experience we have had, and the knowledge we have gained, we must, unless we make a waste of wisdom, be strongly impressed with the advantage, as well as the necessity of strengthening that happy union which had been our salvation, and without which we should have been a ruined people.

that inheritance descend, with every mark of an honorable conveyance. The little it will cost, compared with the worth of the states, the greatness of the object, and the value of the national character, will be a profitable exchange.

But that which must more forcibly strike a thoughtful, penetrating mind, and which includes and renders easy all inferior concerns, is the UNION OF THE STATES. On this our great national character depends. It is this which must give us importance abroad and security at home. It is through this only that we are, or can be, nationally known in the world ; it is the flag of the United States which renders our ships and commerce safe on the seas, or in a foreign port. Our Mediterranean passes must be obtained under the same style. All our treaties, whether of alliance, peace, or commerce, are formed under the sovereignty of the United States, and Europe knows us by no other name or title.

The division of the empire into states is for our own convenience, but abroad this distinction ceases. The affairs of each state are local. They can go no further than to itself. And were the whole worth of even the richest of them expended in revenue, it would not be sufficient to support sovereignty against a foreign attack. In short, we have no other national sovereignty than as United States. It would even be fatal for us if we had — too expensive to be maintained, and impossible to be supported. Individuals, or individual states, may call themselves what they please ; but the world, and especially the world of enemies, is not to be held in awe by the whistling of a name. Sovereignty must have power to protect all the parts that compose and constitute it : and as UNITED STATES we are equal to the importance of the title, but otherwise we are not. Our union, well and wisely regulated and cemented, is the cheapest way of being great — the easiest way of being powerful, and the happiest invention in government which the circumstances of America can admit of. — Because it collects from each state, that which, by being inadequate, can be of no use to it, and forms an aggregate that serves for all.

The states of Holland are an unfortunate instance of the effects of individual sovereignty. Their disjointed condition exposes them to numerous intrigues, losses, calamities, and enemies ; and the almost impossibility of bringing their measures to a decision, and that decision into execution, is to them, and would be to us, a source of endless misfortune.

It is with confederated states as with individuals in society ; something must be yielded up to make the whole secure. In this view of things we gain by what we give, and draw an annual interest greater than the capital. — I ever feel myself hurt when I hear the union, that great palladium of our liberty and safety, the least irreverently spoken of. It is the most sacred thing in the constitution of America, and that which every man should be most proud and tender of. Our citizenship in the United States is our national character. Our citizenship in any particular state is only our local distinction. By the latter we are known at home, by the former to the world. Our great title is AMERICANS — our inferior one varies with the place.

It was the cause of America that made me an author. The force with which it struck my mind, and the dangerous condition the country appeared to me in, by courting an impossible and an unnatural reconciliation with those who were determined to reduce her, instead of striking out into the only line that could cement and save her, A DECLARATION OF INDEPENDENCE, made it impossible for me, feeling as I did, to be silent : and if, in the course of more than seven years, I have rendered her any service, I have likewise added something to the reputation of literature, by freely and disinterestedly

employing it in the great cause of mankind, and showing that there may be genius without prostitution.

But as the scenes of war are closed, and every man
preparing for home and happier times, I therefore take
my leave of the subject.   I have most sincerely followed it from beginning to end, and through all its
turns and windings : and whatever country I may hereafter be in, I shall always feel an honest pride at the part
I have taken and acted, and a gratitude to nature and
providence for putting it in my power to be of some
use to mankind.

COMMON SENSE

PHILADELPHIA, April 19, 1783

RIGHTS OF MAN

(1791)

PART FIRST

Among the incivilities by which nations or individuals provoke and irritate each other, Mr. Burke's pamphlet on the French Revolution is an extraordinary instance. Neither the people of France, nor the National Assembly, were troubling themselves about the affairs of England, or the English Parliament ; and that Mr. Burke should commence an unprovoked attack upon them, both in Parliament and in public, is a conduct that cannot be pardoned on the score of manners, nor justified on that of policy. There is scarcely an epithet of abuse to be found in the English language, with which Mr. Burke has not loaded the French nation and the National Assembly. Every thing which rancor, prejudice, ignorance, or knowledge could suggest, are poured forth in the copious fury of near four hundred pages. In the strain and on the plan Mr. Burke was writing, he might have written on to as many thousands. When the tongue or the pen is let loose in a frenzy of passion, it is the man and not the subject that becomes exhausted.

Not sufficiently content with abusing the National Assembly, a great part of his work is taken up with abusing Dr. Price (one of the best-hearted men that lives), and the two societies in England known by the name of the Revolution Society, and the Society for Constitutional Information.

Dr. Price had preached a sermon on the 4th of November, 1789, being the anniversary of what is called in England the Revolution, which took place in 1688. Mr. Burke, speaking of this sermon, says, "The political divine proceeds dogmatically to assert that, by the principles of the Revolution, the people of England have acquired three fundamental rights :

"1. To choose our own governors.

"2. To cashier them for misconduct.

"3. To frame a government for ourselves."

Dr. Price does not say that the right to do these things exists in this or in that person, or in this or in that description of persons, but that it exists in the *whole* ; that it is a right resident in the nation. Mr. Burke, on the contrary, denies that such a right exists in the nation, either in whole or in part, or that it exists any where ; and, what is still more strange and marvelous, he says, "that the people of England utterly disclaim such a right, and that they will resist the practical assertion of it with their lives and fortunes."

That men should take up arms, and spend their lives and fortunes, *not* to maintain their rights, but to maintain they have *not* rights, is an entirely new species of discovery, and suited to the paradoxical genius of Mr. Burke.

The method which Mr. Burke takes to prove that the people of England had no such rights, and that such rights do not now exist in the nation, either in whole or in part, or any where at all, is of the same marvelous and monstrous kind with what he has already said ; for his arguments are, that the persons, or the generation of persons, in whom they did exist, are dead, and with them the right is dead also.

To prove this, he quotes a declaration made by Parliament about a hundred years ago, to William and Mary, in these words : "The Lords Spiritual and Temporal, and Commons, do, in the name of the people aforesaid," (meaning the people of England then living) "most humbly and faithfully *submit* themselves, their *heirs* and *posterities*, for EVER." He also quotes a clause of another act of Parliament made in the same reign, the terms of which, he says, "bind us," (meaning the people of that day) "our *heirs* and our *posterity*, to *them*, their *heirs* and *posterity*, to the end of time."

There never did, there never will, and there never can exist a parliament, or any description of men, or any generation of men, in any country, possessed of the right or the power of binding and controlling posterity to the "*end of time*," or of commanding for ever how the world shall be governed, or who shall govern it ; and therefore, all such clauses, acts or declarations, by which the makers of them attempt to do what they have neither the right nor the power to do, nor the power to execute, are in themselves null and void.

Every age and generation must be as free to act for itself, *in all cases*, as the ages and generations which preceded it.   The vanity and presumption of governing beyond the grave, is the most ridiculous and insolent of all tyrannies.

Man has no property in man ; neither has any generation a property in the generations which are to follow.   The Parliament or the people of 1688, or of any other period, had no more right to dispose of the people of the present day, or to bind or to control them *in any shape whatever*, than the Parliament or the people of the present day have to dispose of, bind, or control those who are to live a hundred or a thousand years hence.

Every generation is, and must be, competent to all the purposes which its occasions require.   It is the living, and not the dead, that are to be accommodated. When man ceases to be, his power and his wants cease with him ; and having no longer any participation in the concerns of this world, he has no longer any authority in directing who shall be its governors, or how its government shall be organized, or how administered.

There was a time when kings disposed of their crowns by will upon their death-beds, and consigned the people, like beasts of the field, to whatever successor they appointed. This is now so exploded as scarcely to be remembered, and so monstrous as hardly to be believed.

Those who have quitted the world, and those who are not yet arrived in it, are as remote from each other, as the utmost stretch of moral imagination can conceive. What possible obligation, then, can exist between them ; what rule or principle can be laid down, that two nonentities, the one out of existence, and the other not in, and who never can meet in this world, that the one should control the other to the end of time ?

In England, it is said that money cannot be taken out of the pockets of the people without their consent. But who authorized, or who could authorize the Parliament of 1688 to control and take away the freedom of posterity, and limit and confine their right of acting in certain cases for ever, who were not in existence to give or to withhold their consent ?

The Parliament of 1688 might as well have passed an act to have authorized themselves to live for ever as to make their authority to live for ever. All therefore that can be said of them is, that they are a formality of words, of as much import as if those who used them had addressed a congratulation to themselves, and in the oriental style of antiquity, had said, O Parliament, live for ever !

The circumstances of the world are continually changing, and the opinions of men change also ; and as government is for the living, and not for the dead, it is the living only that has any right in it. That which may be thought right and found convenient in one age, may be thought wrong and found inconvenient in another. In such cases, who is to decide, the living, or the dead ?

While I am writing this, there are accidentally before me some proposals for a declaration of rights by the Marquis de Lafayette (I ask his pardon for using his former address, and do it only for distinction's sake) to the National Assembly, on the 11th of July, 1789, three days before the taking of the Bastille, and I cannot but be struck by observing how opposite the sources are from which that gentleman and Mr. Burke draw their principles.

Instead of referring to musty records and moldy parchments to prove that the rights of the living are lost, "renounced and abdicated for ever," by those who are now no more, as Mr. Burke has done, M. de Lafayette applies to the living world, and emphatically says : "Call to mind the sentiments which nature has engraved in the heart of every citizen, and which take a new force when they are solemnly recognized by all : For a nation to love liberty, it is sufficient that she knows it ; and to be free, it is sufficient that she wills it."

It was not against Louis XVI, but against the despotic principles of the government, that the French nation revolted. These principles had not their origin in him, but in the original establishment, many centuries back ; and they were become too deeply rooted to be removed, and the Augean stable of parasites and plunderers too abominably filthy to be cleansed, by anything short of a complete and universal revolution.

The natural moderation of Louis XVI contributed nothing to alter the hereditary despotism of the monarchy. All the tyrannies of the former reigns, acted under that hereditary despotism, were still liable to be revived in the hands of a successor. It was not the respite of a reign that would satisfy France, enlightened as she was then become.

A casual discontinuance of the *practise* of despotism, is not a discontinuance of its *principles* ; the former depends on the virtue of the individual who is in immediate possession of power ; the latter, on the virtue and fortitude of the nation. In the case of Charles I and

James II of England, the revolt was against the personal despotism of the men ; whereas in France, it was
against the hereditary despotism of the established government.

But there are many points of view in which this Revolution may be considered. When despotism has established itself for ages in a country, as in France, it is not
in the person of the king only that it resides. It has
the appearance of being so in show, and in nominal authority ; but it is not so in practise, and in fact. It has
its standard everywhere.

Every office and department has its despotism,
founded upon custom and usage. Every place has its
Bastille, and every Bastille its despot. The original
hereditary despotism, resident in the person of the king,
divides and subdivides itself into a thousand shapes and
forms, till at last the whole of it is acted by deputation.

This was the case in France ; and against this species
of despotism, proceeding on through an endless laby-
rinth of office till the source of it is scarcely perceptible,
there is no mode of redress. It strengthens itself by
assuming the appearance of duty, and tyrannizes under
the pretense of obeying.

From his violence and his grief, his silence on some
points, and his excess on others, it is difficult not to
believe that Mr. Burke is sorry, extremely sorry, that
arbitrary power, the power of the Pope, and the Bastille,
are pulled down.

Not one glance of compassion, not one commiserat-
ing reflection, that I can find throughout his book,
has he bestowed on those who lingered out the most
wretched of lives, a life without hope, in the most miserable of prisons.

It is painful to behold a man employing his talents
to corrupt himself. Nature has been kinder to Mr.
Burke than he is to her. He is not affected by the

reality of distress touching his heart, but by the showy resemblage of it striking his imagination. He pities the plumage, but forgets the dying bird.

Before anything can be reasoned upon to a conclusion, certain facts, principles, or data, to reason from, must be established, admitted, or denied. Mr. Burke, with his usual outrage, abuses the *Declaration of the Rights of Man,* published by the National Assembly of France, as the basis on which the Constitution of France is built. This he calls "paltry and blurred sheets of paper about the rights of man."

Does Mr. Burke mean to deny that *man* has any rights ? If he does, then he must mean that there are no such things as rights any where, and that he has none himself ; for who is there in the world but man ? But if Mr. Burke means to admit that man has rights, the question then will be, what are those rights, and how came man by them originally ?

It is to be observed, that all the religions known in the world are founded, so far as they relate to man, on the *unity of man,* as being all of one degree. Whether in heaven or in hell, or in whatever state man may be supposed to exist hereafter, the good and the bad are the only distinctions. Nay, even the laws of governments are obliged to slide into this principle, by making degrees to consist in crimes and not in persons.

It is one of the greatest of all truths, and of the highest advantage to cultivate. By considering man in this light, and by instructing him to consider himself in this light, it places him in a close connection with all his duties, whether to his Creator or to the creation, of which he is a part ; and it is only when he forgets his origin, or, to use a more fashionable phrase, his *birth and family,* that he becomes dissolute.

It is not among the least of the evils of the present existing governments in all parts of Europe, that man, considered as man, is thrown back to a vast distance from his Maker, and the artificial chasm filled up by a succession of barriers, or a sort of turnpike gates, through which he has to pass.

I will quote Mr. Burke's catalogue of barriers that he has set up between man and his Maker. Putting himself in the character of a herald, he says — "We fear God — we look with *awe* to kings — with affection to parliaments — with duty to magistrates — with reverence to priests, and with respect to nobility." Mr. Burke has forgotten to put in "*chivalry*." He has also forgotten to put in Peter.

The duty of man is not a wilderness of turnpike gates, through which he is to pass by tickets from one to the other. It is plain and simple, and consists but of two points. His duty to God, which every man must feel ; and with respect to his neighbor, to do as he would be done by. If those to whom power is delegated do well, they will be respected; if not, they will be despised ; and with regard to those to whom no power is delegated, but who assume it, the rational world can know nothing of them.

Man did not enter into society to become *worse* than he was before, nor to have fewer rights than he had before, but to have those rights better secured. His natural rights are the foundation of all his civil rights. But in order to pursue this distinction with more precision, it is necessary to make the different qualities of natural and civil rights.

A few words will explain this. Natural rights are those which appertain to man in right of his existence. Of this kind are all the intellectual rights, or rights of the mind, and also all those rights of acting as an individual for his own comfort and happiness, which are not injurious to the natural rights of others. Civil rights are those which appertain to man in right of his being a member of society.

Every civil right has for its foundation some natural

right pre-existing in the individual, but to the enjoyment of which his individual power is not, in all cases, sufficiently competent. Of this kind are all those which relate to security and protection.

From this short review, it will be easy to distinguish between that class of natural rights which man retains after entering into society, and those which he throws into the common stock as a member of society.

The natural rights which are not retained, are all those in which, though the right is perfect in the individual, the power to execute them is defective. They answer not his purpose. A man, by natural right, has a right to judge in his own cause; and so far as the right of the mind is concerned, he never surrenders it : but what availeth it him to judge, if he has not power to redress ? He therefore deposits his right in the common stock of society, and takes the arm of society, of which he is a part, in preference and in addition to his own. Society *grants* him nothing. Every man is proprietor in society, and draws on the capital as a matter of right.

In casting our eyes over the world, it is extremely easy to distinguish the governments which have arisen out of society, or out of the social compact, from those which have not : but to place this in a clearer light than what a single glance may afford, it will be proper to take a review of the several sources from which the governments have arisen, and on which they have been founded.

They may be all comprehended under three heads. First, superstition. Secondly, power. Thirdly, the common interests of society, and the common rights of man.

The first was a government of priestcraft, the second of conquerors, and the third of reason.

When a set of artful men pretended, through the medium of oracles, to hold intercourse with the Deity, as familiarly as they now march up the back-stairs in European courts, the world was completely under the government of superstition. The oracles were consulted, and whatever they were made to say, became the law ; and this sort of government lasted as long as this sort of superstition lasted.

After these a race of conquerors arose, whose government, like that of William the Conqueror, was founded in power, and the sword assumed the name of a sceptre. Governments thus established, last as long as the power to support them lasts ; but that they might avail themselves of every engine in their favor, they united fraud to force, and set up an idol which they called *Divine Right*, and which, in imitation of the Pope, who affects to be spiritual and temporal, and in contradiction to the Founder of the Christian religion, twisted itself afterwards into an idol of another shape, called *Church and State*. The key of St. Peter, and the key of the Treasury, became quartered on one another, and the wondering, cheated multitude worshipped the invention.

It has been thought a considerable advance toward establishing the principles of freedom, to say, that government is a compact between those who govern and those who are governed : but this cannot be true, because it is putting the effect before the cause ; for as man must have existed before governments existed, there necessarily was a time when governments did not exist, and consequently there could originally exist no governors to form such a compact with.

The fact therefore must be, that the *individuals themselves*, each in his own personal and sovereign right, *entered into a compact with each other* to produce a government : and this is the only mode in which governments have a right to arise, and the only principle on which they have a right to exist.

To possess ourselves of a clear idea of what government is, or ought to be, we must trace it to its origin. In doing this, we shall easily discover that governments must have arisen, either *out* of the people, or *over* the people.

A constitution is not a thing in name only, but in fact. It has not an ideal, but a real existence ; and wherever it cannot be produced in a visible form, there is none. A constitution is a thing *antecedent* to a government, and a government is only the creature of a constitution. The constitution of a country is not the act of its government, but of the people constituting a government.

It is the body of elements, to which you can refer, and quote article by article ; and which contains the principles on which the government shall be established, the manner in which it shall be organized, the powers it shall have, the mode of elections, the duration of parliaments, or by what other name such bodies may be called ; the powers which the executive part of the government shall have ; and, in fine, every thing that relates to the complete organization of a civil government, and the principles on which it shall act, and by which it shall be bound.

A constitution, therefore, is to a government, what the laws made afterwards by that government are to a court of judicature. The court of judicature does not make the laws, neither can it alter them ; it only acts in conformity to the laws made : and the government is in like manner governed by the constitution.

I readily perceive the reason why Mr. Burke declined going into the comparison between the English and French constitutions, because he could not but perceive, when he sat down to the task, that no such thing as a constitution existed on his side the question. His book is certainly bulky enough to have contained all he could say on this subject, and it would have been the best manner in which people could have judged of their separate merits.

Why then has he declined the only thing that was worth while to write upon ? It was the strongest ground he could take, if the advantages were on his side ; but the weakest, if they were not ; and his declining to take it, is either a sign that he could not possess it, or could not maintain it.

The present National Assembly of France is, strictly speaking, the personal social compact. The members of it are the delegates of the nation in its *original* character ; future assemblies will be the delegates of the nation in its *organized* character.

The authority of the present Assembly is different to what the authority of future assemblies will be. The authority of the present one is to form a constitution; the authority of future assemblies will be to legislate according to the principles and forms prescribed in that constitution ; and if experience should hereafter show that alterations, amendments, or additions are necessary, the constitution will point out the mode by which such things shall be done, and not leave it to the discretionary power of the future government.

A government on the principles on which constitutional governments, arising out of society are established, cannot have the right of altering itself. If it had, it would be arbitrary. It might make itself what it pleased ; and wherever such a right is set up, it shows that there is no constitution.

The right of reform is in the nation in its original character, and the constitutional method would be by a general convention elected for the purpose. There is, moreover, a paradox in the idea of vitiated bodies reforming themselves.

One of the first works of the National Assembly, instead of vindictive proclamations, as has been the case with other governments, was to publish a Declaration of the Rights of Man, as the basis on which the new Constitution was to be built, and which is here subjoined.

DECLARATION OF THE
RIGHTS OF MAN AND OF CITIZENS
BY THE NATIONAL ASSEMBLY OF FRANCE

"The Representatives of the people of FRANCE, formed into a NATIONAL ASSEMBLY, considering that ignorance, neglect, or contempt of human rights, are the sole causes of public misfortunes and corruptions of government, have resolved to set forth in a solemn declaration, these natural, imprescriptible, and unalienable rights : that this declaration, being constantly present to the minds of the members of the body social, they may be ever kept attentive to their rights and their duties : that the acts of the legislative and executive powers of government, being capable of being every moment compared with the end of political institutions, may be more respected : and also, that the future claims of the citizens, being directed by simple and incontestible principles, may always tend to the maintenance of the Constitution, and the general happiness.

"For these reasons the NATIONAL ASSEMBLY doth recognize and declare, in the presence of the Supreme Being, and with the hope of His blessing and favor, the following *sacred* rights of men and of citizens :

"I. *Men are born, and always continue, free, and equal in respect of their rights. Civil distinctions, therefore, can be founded only on public utility.*

"II. *The end of all political associations, is, the preservation of the natural and imprescriptible rights of man ; and these rights are liberty, property, security, and resistance of oppression.*

"III. *The nation is essentially the source of all sovereignty ; nor can any* INDIVIDUAL, *or* ANY BODY OF MEN, *be entitled to any authority which is not expressly derived from it.*

"IV. Political liberty consists in the power of doing whatever does not injure another. The exercise of the natural rights of every man has no other limits than those which are necessary to secure to every *other* man the free exercise of the same rights ; and these limits are determinable only by the law.

"V. The law ought to prohibit only actions hurtful to society. What is not prohibited by the law, should not be hindered ; nor should any one be compelled to that which the law does not require.

"VI. The law is an expression of the will of the community. All citizens have a right to concur, either personally, or by their representatives, in its formation. It should be the same to all, whether it protects or punishes ; and *all being equal in its sight, are equally eligible to all honors, places, and employments, according to their different abilities, without any other distinction than that created by their virtues and talents.*

"VII. No man should be accused, arrested, or held in confinement, except in cases determined by the law, and according to the forms which it has prescribed. All who promote, solicit, execute, or cause to be executed, arbitrary orders, ought to be punished ; and every citizen called upon or apprehended by virtue of the law, ought immediately to obey, and renders himself culpable by resistance.

"VIII. The law ought to impose no other penalties but such as are absolutely and evidently necessary : and no one ought to be punished, but in virtue of a law promulgated before the offense, and legally applied.

"IX. Every man being presumed innocent till he has been convicted, whenever his detention becomes indispensable, all rigor to him, more than is necessary to secure his person, ought to be provided against by the law.

"X. No man ought to be molested on account of his opinions, not even on account of his *religious* opinions, provided his avowal of them does not disturb the public order established by the law.

"XI. The unrestrained communication of thoughts and opinions being one of the most precious rights of man, every citizen may speak, write, and publish freely, provided he is responsible for the abuse of this liberty in cases determined by the law.

"XII. A public force being necessary to give security to the rights of men and of citizens, that force is instituted for the benefit of the community, and not for the particular benefit of the persons with whom it is intrusted.

"XIII. A common contribution being necessary for the support of the public force, and for defraying the other expenses of government, it ought to be divided equally among the members of the community, according to their abilities.

"XIV. Every citizen has a right, either by himself or his representative, to a free voice in determining the necessity of public contributions, the appropriation of them, and their amount, mode of assessment, and duration.

"XV. Every community has a right to demand of all its agents, an account of their conduct.

"XVI. Every community in which a separation of powers and a security of rights is not provided for, wants a constitution.

"XVII. The rights to property being inviolable and sacred, no one ought to be deprived of it, except in cases of evident public necessity, legally ascertained, and on condition of a previous just indemnity."

While the Declaration of Rights was before the National Assembly, some of its members remarked, that if a Declaration of Rights was published, it should be accompanied by a Declaration of Duties. The observation discovered a mind that reflected, and it only erred by not reflecting far enough. A Declaration of Rights is, by reciprocity, a Declaration of Duties also. Whatever is my right as a man, is also the right of another ; and it becomes my duty to guarantee, as well as to possess.

The three first articles are the basis of liberty, as well individual as national ; nor can any country be called free, whose government does not take its beginning from the principles they contain, and continue to preserve them pure ; and the whole of the Declaration of Rights is of more value to the world, and will do more good, than all the laws and statutes that have yet been promulgated.

In the declaratory exordium which prefaces the Declaration of Rights, we see the solemn and majestic spectacle of a nation opening its commission, under the auspices of its Creator, to establish a Government ; a scene so new, and so transcendently unequalled by any thing in the European world, that the name of a revolution is diminutive of its character, and it rises into a regeneration of man.

I will close the subject with the energetic apostrophe of M. de Lafayette — *May this great monument, raised to Liberty, serve as a lesson to the oppressor, and an example to the oppressed !*

CONCLUSION

Reason and Ignorance, the opposites of each other, influence the great bulk of mankind. If either of these can be rendered sufficiently extensive in a country, the machinery of government goes easily on. Reason obeys itself ; and Ignorance submits to whatever is dictated to it.

The two modes of government which prevail in the world, are, *First*, government by election and representation : *Secondly*, government by hereditary succession. The former is generally known by the name of republic ; the latter by that of monarchy and aristocracy.

Those two distinct and opposite forms, erect themselves on the two distinct and opposite bases of Reason and Ignorance. As the exercise of government requires talents and abilities, and as talents and abilities cannot have hereditary descent, it is evident that hereditary succession requires a belief from man, to which his reason cannot subscribe, and which can only be established upon his ignorance ; and the more ignorant any country is, the better it is fitted for this species of government.

On the contrary, government in a well constituted republic, requires no belief from man beyond what his reason can give. He sees the *rationale* of the whole system, its origin and its operation ; and as it is best supported when best understood, the human faculties act with boldness, and acquire, under this form of government, a gigantic manliness.

As, therefore, each of those forms acts on a different base, the one moving freely by the aid of reason, the other by ignorance ; we have next to consider, what it is that gives motion to that species of government which is called mixed government, such as the English, or, as it is sometimes ludicrously styled, a government of *this*, *that*, and *t'other*.

The moving power of this species of government is, of necessity, corruption. However imperfect election and representation may be in mixed governments, they still give exercise to a greater portion of reason than is convenient to the hereditary part ; and therefore it becomes necessary to buy the reason up. A mixed government is an imperfect everything, cementing and

soldering the discordant parts together by corruption,
to act as a whole.

In mixed governments there is no responsibility :
the parts cover each other till responsibility is lost ; and
the corruption which moves the machine, contrives at
the same time its own escape. When it is laid down
as a maxim, that *a king can do no wrong*, it places him
in a state of similar security with that of idiots and persons insane, and responsibility is out of the question
with respect to himself. It then descends upon the
minister, who shelters himself under a majority in
Parliament, which, by places, pensions, and corruption, he can always command ; and that majority justifies itself by the same authority with which it protects
the minister. In this rotary motion, responsibility is
thrown off from the parts, and from the whole.

When there is a part in a government which can do
no wrong, it implies that it does nothing ; and is only
the machine of another power, by whose advice and
direction it acts. What is supposed to be the king in
mixed governments is the cabinet ; and as the cabinet
is always a part of the parliament, and the members
justifying in one character what they advise and act
in another, a mixed government becomes a continual
enigma ; entailing upon a country, by the quantity of
corruption necessary to solder the parts, the expense
of supporting all the forms of government at once, and
finally resolving itself into a government by committee ; in which the advisers, the actors, the approvers,
the justifiers, the persons responsible, and the persons
not responsible, are the same persons.

By this pantomimical contrivance, and change of
scene and character, the parts help each other out in
matters which neither of them singly would assume to
act. When money is to be obtained, the mass of variety apparently dissolves, and a profusion of parlia-
mentary praises passes between the parts. Each ad-

mires with astonishment, the wisdom, the liberality, the disinterestedness of the other ; and all of them breathe a pitying sigh at the burdens of the nation.

But in a well constituted republic, nothing of this soldering, praising, and pitying, can take place ; the representation being equal throughout the country, and complete in itself, however it may be arranged into legislative and executive, they have all one and the same natural source. The parts are not foreigners to each other, like democracy, aristocracy, and monarchy. As there are no discordant distinctions, there is nothing to corrupt by compromise, nor confound by contrivance.

Public measures appeal of themselves to the understanding of the nation, and, resting on their own merits, disown any flattering application to vanity. The continual whine of lamenting the burden of taxes, however successfully it may be practised in mixed governments, is inconsistent with the sense and spirit of a republic. If taxes are necessary, they are of course advantageous ; but if they require an apology, the apology itself implies an impeachment. Why then is man thus imposed upon, or why does he impose upon himself ?

When we survey the wretched condition of man under the monarchical and hereditary systems of government, dragged from his home by one power, or driven by another, and impoverished by taxes more than by enemies, it becomes evident that those systems are bad, and that a general revolution in the principle and construction of governments is necessary.

What is government more than the management of the affairs of a nation ? It is not, and from its nature cannot be, the property of any particular man or family, but of the whole community, at whose expense it is supported ; and though by force or contrivance it has been usurped into an inheritance, the usurpation cannot alter the right of things. Sovereignty, as a matter of right, appertains to the nation only, and not to any individual ; and a nation has at all times an inherent indefeasible right to abolish any form of government it finds inconvenient, and establish such as accords with its interest, disposition, and happiness.

In these principles, there is nothing to throw a nation into confusion by inflaming ambition. They are calculated to call forth wisdom and abilities, and to exercise them for the public good, and not for the emolument or aggrandizement of particular descriptions of men or families. Monarchial sovereignty, the enemy of mankind, and the source of misery, is abolished ; and sovereignty itself is restored to its natural and original place, the nation. Were this the case throughout Europe, the cause of wars would be taken away.

It is attributed to Henry IV of France, a man of an enlarged and benevolent heart, that he proposed, about the year 1610, a plan of abolishing war in Europe. The plan consisted in constituting an European Congress, or as the French authors style it, a Pacific Republic ; by appointing delegates from the several nations, who were to act as a court of arbitration in any disputes that might arise between nation and nation. Had such a plan been adopted at the time it was proposed, the taxes of England and France, as two of the parties, would have been at least ten millions sterling annually to each nation less than they were at the commencement of the French Revolution.

To conceive a cause why such a plan has not been adopted (and that instead of a congress for the purpose of *preventing* war, it has been called only to *terminate* a war, after fruitless expense of several years), it will be necessary to consider the interest of governments as a distinct interest to that of nations.

Whatever is the cause of taxes to a nation, becomes also the means of revenue to a government. Every war terminates with an addition of taxes, and consequently with an addition of revenue ; and in any event of war, in the manner they are now commenced and concluded, the power and interest of governments are increased.

War, therefore, from its productiveness, as it easily furnishes the pretence of necessity for taxes and appointments to places and offices, becomes a principal part of the system of old governments ; and to establish any mode to abolish war, however advantageous it might be to nations, would be to take from such government the most lucrative of its branches. The frivolous matters upon which war is made, show the disposition and avidity of governments to uphold the system of war, and betray the motives upon which they act.

Why are not republics plunged into war, but because the nature of their government does not admit of an interest distinct from that of the nation ? Even Holland, though an ill-constructed republic, and with a commerce extending over the world, existed nearly a century without war : and the instant the form of government was changed in France, the republican principles of peace and domestic prosperity and economy arose with the new Government ; and the same consequences would follow the same causes in other nations.

As war is the system of government on the old construction, the animosity which nations reciprocally entertain, is nothing more than what the policy of their governments excites, to keep up the spirit of the system. Each government accuses the other of perfidy, intrigue, and ambition, as a means of heating the imagination of their respective nations, and increasing them to hostilities. Man is not the enemy of man, but through the medium of a false system of government. Instead, therefore, of exclaiming against the ambition of kings, the exclamation should be directed against the

principle of such governments ; and instead of seeking
to reform the individual, the wisdom of a nation should
apply itself to reform the system.

Whether the forms and maxims of governments
which are still in practise, were adapted to the condition of the world at the period they were established,
is not in this case the question. The older they are,
the less correspondence can they have with the present
state of things. Time, and change of circumstances
and opinions, have the same progressive effect in ren-
dering modes of government obsolete, as they have
upon customs and manners. Agriculture, commerce,
manufactures, and the tranquil arts, by which the prosperity of nations is best promoted, require a different
system of government, and a different species of knowledge to direct its operations, than what might have
been required in the former condition of the world.

As it is not difficult to perceive, from the enlightened state of mankind, that hereditary governments
are verging to their decline, and that revolutions on
the broad basis of national sovereignty, and government by representation, are making their way in Europe, it would be an act of wisdom to anticipate their
approach, and produce revolutions by reason and accommodation, rather than commit them to the issue of
convulsions.

From what we now see, nothing of reform on the
political world ought to be held improbable. It is an
age of revolutions, in which every thing may be looked
for. The intrigue of courts, by which the system of
war is kept up, may provoke a confederation of nations
to abolish it : and an European Congress, to patronize
the progress of free government, and promote the civilization of nations with each other, is an event nearer
in probability, than once were the revolutions and alliance of France and America.

RIGHTS OF MAN

(1792)

PART SECOND

What Archimedes said of the mechanical powers, may be applied to reason and liberty : *"Had we,"* said he, *"a place to stand upon, we might raise the world."*

The Revolution of America presented in politics what was only theory in mechanics. So deeply rooted were all the governments of the old world, and so effectually had the tyranny and the antiquity of habit established itself over the mind, that no beginning could be made in Asia, Africa, or Europe, to reform the political condition of man. Freedom had been hunted round the globe ; reason was considered as rebellion ; and the slavery of fear had made men afraid to think.

But such is the irresistible nature of truth, that all it asks, and all it wants, is the liberty of appearing. The sun needs no inscription to distinguish him from darkness ; and no sooner did the American governments display themselves to the world, than despotism felt a shock, and man began to contemplate redress.

The independence of America, considered merely as a separation from England, would have been a matter but of little importance, had it not been accompanied by a revolution in the principles and practise of governments. She made a stand, not for herself only, but for the world, and looked beyond the advantages herself could receive. Even the Hessian, though hired to fight against her, may live to bless his defeat ; and England, condemning the viciousness of its government, rejoice in its miscarriage.

As America was the only spot in the political world,

where the principles of universal reformation could begin, so also was it the best in the natural world. An assemblage of circumstances conspired, not only to give birth, but to add gigantic maturity to its principles.

The scene which that country presents to the eye of a spectator, has something in it which generates and encourages great ideas. Nature appears to him in magnitude. The mighty objects he beholds, act upon his mind by enlarging it, and he partakes of the greatness he contemplates. Its first settlers were emigrants from different European nations, and of diversified professions of religion, retiring from the governmental persecutions of the old world, and meeting in the new, not as enemies, but as brothers. The wants which necessarily accompany the cultivation of a wilderness, produced among them a state of society, which countries, long harassed by the quarrels and intrigues of governments, had neglected to cherish. In such a situation man becomes what he ought. He sees his species, not with the inhuman idea of a natural enemy, but as kindred ; and the example shows to the artificial world, that man must go back to nature for information.

From the rapid progress which America makes in every species of improvement, it is rational to conclude, that if the governments of Asia, Africa, and Europe, had begun on a principle similar to that of America, or had not been very early corrupted therefrom, that those countries must, by this time, have been in a far superior condition to what they are. Age after age has passed away, for no other purpose than to behold their wretchedness. Could we suppose a spectator who knew nothing of the world, and who was put into it merely to make his observations, he would take a great part of the old world to be new, just struggling with the difficulties and hardships of an infant settlement. He could not suppose that the hordes of miserable poor, with which old countries abound, could be any other than those who had not yet had time to provide for themselves. Little would he think they were the consequence of what in such countries is called government.

If, from the more wretched parts of the old world, we look at those which are in an advanced stage of improvement, we still find the greedy hand of government thrusting itself into every corner and crevice of industry, and grasping the spoil of the multitude. Invention is continually exercised, to furnish new pretenses for revenue and taxation. It watches prosperity as its prey, and permits none to escape without tribute.

If systems of government can be introduced, less expensive, and more productive of general happiness, than those which have existed, all attempts to oppose their progress will in the end be fruitless. Reason, like time, will make its own way, and prejudice will fall in a combat with interest. If universal peace, civilization, and commerce, are ever to be the happy lot of man, it cannot be accomplished but by a revolution in the system of governments. All the monarchical governments are military. War is their trade, plunder and revenue their objects. While such governments continue, peace has not the absolute security of a day.

What is the history of all monarchical governments, but a disgustful picture of human wretchedness, and the accidental respite of a few years' repose? Wearied with war, and tired with human butchery, they sat down to rest, and called it peace.

Conquest and tyranny, at some early period, dispossessed man of his rights, and he is now recovering them. And as the tide of all human affairs has its ebb and flow in directions contrary to each other, so also is it in this. Government founded on a *moral theory,* *on a system of universal peace, on the indefeasible,*

hereditary rights of man, is now revolving from West
to East, by a stronger impulse than the government
of the sword revolved from East to West. It interests
not particular individuals, but nations, in its progress,
and promises a new era to the human race.

The danger to which the success of revolutions is
most exposed, is that of attempting them before the
principles on which they proceed, and the advantages
to result from them, are sufficiently seen and understood. Almost everything appertaining to the circumstances of a nation, has been absorbed and confounded
under the general and mysterious word *government.*
Though it avoids taking to its account the errors it
commits, and the mischiefs it occasions, it fails not to
arrogate to itself whatever has the appearance of prosperity. It robs industry of its honors, by pedantically
making itself the cause of its effects ; and purloins
from the general character of man, the merits that
appertain to him as a social being.

It may therefore be of use, in this day of revolutions, to discriminate between those things which are
the effect of government, and those which are not.
This will best be done by taking a review of society
and civilization, and the consequences resulting therefrom, as things distinct from what are called governments. By beginning with this investigation, we shall
be able to assign effects to their proper cause, and ana-
lyze the mass of common errors.

Great part of that order which reigns among mankind is not the effect of government. It had its origin
in the principles of society and the natural constitution of man. It existed prior to government, and
would exist if the formality of government was abolished. The mutual dependence and reciprocal interest
which man has upon man, and all parts of a civilized
community upon each other, create that great chain of

connection which holds it together. The landholder, the farmer, the manufacturer, the merchant, the tradesman, and every occupation, prospers by the aid which each receives from the other, and from the whole. Common interest regulates their concerns, and forms their laws; and the laws which common usage ordains, have a greater influence than the laws of government. In fine, society performs for itself almost every thing which is ascribed to government.

To understand the nature and quantity of government proper for man, it is necessary to attend to his character. As Nature created him for social life, she fitted him for the station she intended. In all cases she made his natural wants greater than his individual powers. No one man is capable, without the aid of society, of supplying his own wants; and those wants acting upon every individual, impel the whole of them into society, as naturally as gravitation acts to a center.

But she has gone further. She has not only forced man into society, by a diversity of wants, which the reciprocal aid of each other can supply, but she has implanted in him a system of social affections, which, though not necessary to his existence, are essential to his happiness. There is no period in life when this love for society ceases to act. It begins and ends with our being.

If we examine, with attention, into the composition and constitution of man, the diversity of his wants, and the diversity of talents in different men for reciprocally accommodating the wants of each other, his propensity to society, and consequently to preserve the advantages resulting from it, we shall easily discover that a great part of what is called government is mere imposition.

Government is no farther necessary than to supply the few cases to which society and civilization are not conveniently competent; and instances are not wanting to show, that every thing which government can usefully add thereto, has been performed by the common consent of society, without government.

For upward of two years from the commencement of the American War, and to a longer period in several of the American states, there were no established forms of government. The old governments had been abolished, and the country was too much occupied in defense, to employ its attention in establishing new governments ; yet during this interval, order and harmony were preserved as inviolate as in any country in Europe.

There is a natural aptness in man, and more so in society, because it embraces a greater variety of abilities and resources, to accommodate itself to whatever situation it is in. The instant formal government is abolished, society begins to act. A general association takes place, and common interest produces common security.

So far is it from being true, as has been pretended, that the abolition of any formal government is the dissolution of society, that it acts by a contrary impulse, and brings the latter the closer together. All that part of its organization which it had committed to its government, devolves again upon itself, and acts through its medium.

When men, as well from natural instinct, as from reciprocal benefits, have habituated themselves to social and civilized life, there is always enough of its principles in practise to carry them through any changes they may find necessary or convenient to make in their government. In short, man is so naturally a creature of society, that it is almost impossible to put him out of it.

Formal government makes but a small part of civilized life ; and when even the best that human wisdom can devise is established, it is a thing more in name and idea, than in fact. It is to the great and fundamental principles of society and civilization — to the common usage universally consented to, and mutually and reciprocally maintained — to the unceasing circulation of interest, which, passing through its million channels, invigorates the whole mass of civilized man — it is to these things, infinitely more than to any thing which even the best instituted government can perform, that the safety and prosperity of the individual and of the whole depends.

The more perfect civilization is, the less occasion has it for government, because the more does it regulate its own affairs, and govern itself ; but so contrary is the practise of old governments to the reason of the case, that the expenses of them increase in the proportion they ought to diminish. It is but few general laws that civilized life requires, and those of such common usefulness, that whether they are enforced by the forms of government or not, the effect will be nearly the same. If we consider what the principles are that first condense men into society, and what the motives that regulate their mutual intercourse afterwards, we shall find, by the time we arrive at what is called government, that nearly the whole of the business is performed by the natural operation of the parts upon each other.

Man, with respect to all those matters, is more a creature of consistency than he is aware, or that governments would wish him to believe. All the great laws of society are laws of nature. Those of trade and commerce, whether with respect to the intercourse of individuals, or of nations, are laws of mutual and reciprocal interest. They are followed and obeyed because it is the interest of the parties so to do, and not on account of any formal laws their governments may impose or interpose.

But how often is the natural propensity to society

disturbed or destroyed by the operations of government. When the latter, instead of being ingrafted on the principles of the former, assumes to exist for itself, and acts by partialities of favor and oppression, it becomes the cause of the mischiefs it ought to prevent.

If we look back to the riots and tumults, which at various times have happened in England, we shall find, that they did not proceed from the want of a government, but that government was itself the generating cause; instead of consolidating society, it divided it; it deprived it of its natural cohesion, and engendered discontents and disorders, which otherwise would not have existed.

In those associations which men promiscuously form for the purpose of trade, or of any concern, in which government is totally out of the question, and in which they act merely on the principles of society, we see how naturally the various parties unite; and this shows, by comparison, that governments, so far from being always the cause or means of order, are often the destruction of it. The riots of 1780 had no other source than the remains of those prejudices, which the government itself had encouraged. But with respect to England there are also other causes.

Excess and inequality of taxation, however disguised in the means, never fail to appear in their effects. As a great mass of the community are thrown thereby into poverty and discontent, they are constantly on the brink of commotion; and deprived, as they unfortunately are, of the means of information, are easily heated to outrage. Whatever the apparent cause of any riots may be, the real one is always want of happiness. It shows that something is wrong in the system of government, that injures the felicity by which society is to be preserved.

But as fact is superior to reasoning, the instance of America presents itself to confirm these observations.

If there is a country in the world, where concord, ac-cording to common calculation, would be least ex-pected, it is America. Made up, as it is, of people from different nations, accustomed to different forms and habits of government, speaking different languages, and more different in their modes of worship, it would appear that the union of such a people was impractica-ble ; but by the simple operation of constructing gov-ernment on the principles of society and the rights of man, every difficulty retires, and all the parts are brought into cordial unison. There the poor are not oppressed, the rich are not privileged. Industry is not mortified by the splendid extravagance of a court riot-ing at its expense. Their taxes are few, because their government is just ; and as there is nothing to render them wretched, there is nothing to engender riots and tumults.

A metaphysical man, like Mr. Burke, would have tor-tured his invention to discover how such a people could be governed. He would have supposed that some must be managed by fraud, others by force, and all by some contrivance ; that genius must be hired to impose upon ignorance, and show and parade to fasci-nate the vulgar. Lost in the abundance of his re-searches, he would have resolved and re-resolved, and finally overlooked the plain and easy road that lay directly before him.

One of the great advantages of the American Revo-lution has been, that it led to a discovery of the prin-ciples, and laid open the imposition, of governments. All the revolutions till then had been worked within the atmosphere of a court, and never on the great floor of a nation. The parties were always of the class of courtiers ; and whatever was their rage for reforma-tion, they carefully preserved that fraud of the pro-fession.

In all cases they took care to represent government

as a thing made up of mysteries, which only themselves
understood, and they hid from the understanding of
the nation, the only thing that was beneficial to know,
namely, *That government is nothing more than a national association acting on the principles of society.*

The representative system takes society and civilization for its basis ; nature, reason, and experience for
its guide.

Experience, in all ages, and in all countries, has demonstrated, that it is impossible to control Nature in her
distribution of mental powers. She gives them as she
pleases. Whatever is the rule by which she, apparently to us, scatters them among mankind, that rule
remains a secret to man. It would be as ridiculous to
attempt to fix the hereditaryship of human beauty, as
of wisdom.

Whatever wisdom constituently is, it is like a seed-
less plant ; it may be reared when it appears, but it
cannot be voluntarily produced. There is always a
sufficiency somewhere in the general mass of society
for all purposes ; but with respect to the parts of society, it is continually changing its place. It rises in
one today, in another tomorrow, and has most probably visited in rotation every family of the earth, and
again withdrawn.

As this is the order of nature, the order of government must necessarily follow it, or government will,
as we see it does, degenerate into ignorance. The
hereditary system, therefore, is as repugnant to human
wisdom, as to human rights, and is as absurd, as it is
unjust.

As the republic of letters brings forward the best
literary productions, by giving to genius a fair and
universal chance ; so the representative system of government is calculated to produce the wisest laws, by
collecting wisdom where it can be found. I smile to
myself when I contemplate the ridiculous insignificance

into which literature and all the sciences would sink, were they made hereditary; and I carry the same idea into governments. An hereditary governor is as inconsistent as an hereditary author. I know not whether Homer or Euclid had sons; but I will venture an opinion, that if they had, and had left their works unfinished, those sons could not have completed them.

It appears to general observation, that revolutions create genius and talents; but those events do no more than bring them forward. There is existing in man, a mass of sense lying in a dormant state, and which, unless something excites it to action, will descend with him, in that condition, to the grave. As it is to the advantage of society that the whole of its faculties should be employed, the construction of government ought to be such as to bring forward, by a quiet and regular operation, all that extent of capacity which never fails to appear in revolutions.

This cannot take place in the insipid state of hereditary government, not only because it prevents, but because it operates to benumb. When the mind of a nation is bowed down by any political superstition in its government, such as hereditary succession is, it loses a considerable portion of its powers on all other subjects and objects.

Hereditary succession requires the same obedience to ignorance, as to wisdom; and when once the mind can bring itself to pay this indiscriminate reverence, it descends below the stature of mental manhood. It is fit to be great only in little things. It acts a treachery upon itself, and suffocates the sensations that urge to detection.

Though the ancient governments present to us a miserable picture of the condition of man, there is one which above all others exempts itself from the general description. I mean the democracy of the Athenians. We see more to admire, and less to condemn, in that great, extraordinary people, than in any thing which history affords.

Simple democracy was no other than the common hall of the ancients. It signifies the *form*, as well as the public principle of the government. As these democracies increased in population, and the territory extended, the simple democratical form became unwieldy and impracticable ; and as the system of representation was not known, the consequence was, they either degenerated convulsively into monarchies, or became absorbed into such as then existed.

Had the system of representation been then understood, as it now is, there is no reason to believe that those forms of government, now called monarchical and aristocratical, would ever have taken place. It was the want of some method to consolidate the parts of society, after it became too populous, and too extensive for the simple democratical form, and also the lax and solitary condition of shepherds and herdsmen in other parts of the world, that afforded opportunities to those unnatural modes of government to begin.

Simple democracy was society governing itself without the aid of secondary means. By ingrafting representation upon democracy, we arrive at a system of government capable of embracing and confederating all the various interests and every extent of territory and population ; and that also with advantages as much superior to hereditary government, as the republic of letters is to hereditary literature.

It is on this system that the American government is founded. It is representation ingrafted upon democracy. It has fixed the form by a scale parallel in all cases to the extent of the principle. What Athens was in miniature, America will be in magnitude. The one was the wonder of the ancient world ; the other is becoming the admiration and model of the present. It is the easiest of all the forms of government to be understood, and the most eligible in practise; and excludes at once the ignorance and insecurity of the hereditary mode, and the inconvenience of the simple democracy.

That which is called government, or rather that which we ought to conceive government to be, is no more than some common centre, in which all the parts of society unite. This cannot be accomplished by any method so conducive to the various interests of the community, as by the representative system.

It concentrates the knowledge necessary to the interests of the parts, and of the whole. It places government in a state of constant maturity. It is, as has been already observed, never young, never old. It is subject neither to nonage, nor dotage. It is never in the cradle, nor on crutches. It admits not of a separation between knowledge and power, and is superior, as government always ought to be, to all the accidents of individual man, and is therefore superior to what is called monarchy.

It may not be improper to remind the reader, that the United States of America consist of thirteen separate states, each of which established a government for itself, after the Declaration of Independence, done the fourth of July, 1776. Each state acted independently of the rest, in forming its government; but the same general principle pervades the whole. When the several state governments were formed, they proceeded to form the Federal Government, that acts over the whole in all matters which concern the interest of the whole, or which relate to the intercourse of the several states with each other, or with foreign nations. I will begin with giving an instance from one of the state governments, (that of Pennsylvania) and then proceed to the Federal Government.

The State of Pennsylvania, though nearly of the same extent of territory as England, was then divided into only twelve counties. Each of those counties had elected a committee at the commencement of the dispute with the English Government; and as the city of Philadelphia, which also had its committee, was the most central for intelligence, it became the centre of communication to the several county committees. When it became necessary to proceed to the formation of a government, the Committee of Philadelphia proposed a conference of all the county committees, to be held in that city, and which met the latter end of July 1776.

Though these committees had been elected by the people, they were not elected expressly for the purpose, nor invested with the authority of forming a constitution; and as they could not, consistently with the American idea of rights, assume such a power, they could only confer upon the matter, and put it into a train of operation. The conferees, therefore, did no more than state the case, and recommend to the several counties to elect six representatives for each county, to meet in convention at Philadelphia, with powers to form a constitution, and propose it for public consideration.

This convention, of which Benjamin Franklin was president, having met and deliberated, and agreed upon a constitution, they next ordered it to be published, not as a thing established, but for the consideration of the whole people, their approbation or rejection, and then adjourned to a stated time.

When the time of adjournment was expired, the convention re-assembled, and as the general opinion of the people in approbation of it was then known, the constitution was signed, sealed, and proclaimed on the *authority of the people*; and the original instrument deposited as a public record.

The convention then appointed a day for the general election of the representatives who were to compose the Government, and the time it should commence ; and having done this, they dissolved, and returned to their several homes and occupations.

In this constitution were laid down, first, a declaration of rights. Then followed the form which the Government should have, and the powers it should possess — the authority of the courts of judicature, and of juries — the manner in which elections should be conducted, and the proportion of representatives to the number of electors — the time which each succeeding assembly should continue, which was one year — the mode of levying, and of accounting for the expenditure, of public money — of appointing public officers, etc.

No article of this Constitution could be altered or infringed at the discretion of the Government that was to ensue. It was to that Government a law. But as it would have been unwise to preclude the benefit of experience, and in order also to prevent the accumulation of errors, if any should be found, and to preserve a unison of government with the circumstances of the State at all times, the Constitution provided, that, at the expiration of every seven years, a convention should be elected, for the express purpose of revising the Constitution, and making alterations, additions, or abolitions therein, if any such should be found necessary.

Here we see a regular process — a government issuing out of a constitution, formed by the people in their original character ; and that constitution serving, not only as an authority, but as a law of control to the government. It was the political bible of the State. Scarcely a family was without it. Every member of the Government had a copy ; and nothing was more common when any debate arose on the principle of a bill, or on the extent of any species of authority, than for the members to take the printed Constitution out of their pocket, and read the chapter with which such matter in debate was connected.

Having thus given an instance from one of the states, I will show the proceedings by which the Federal Constitution of the United States arose and was formed.

Congress, at its two first meetings, in September 1774, and May 1775, was nothing more than a deputation from the legislatures of the several provinces, afterwards states; and had no other authority than what arose from common consent, and the necessity of its acting as a public body. In every thing which related to the internal affairs of America, Congress went no farther than to issue recommendations to the several provincial assemblies, who at discretion adopted them or not.

Nothing on the part of Congress was compulsive; yet, in this situation, it was more faithfully and affectionately obeyed, than was any government in Europe. This instance, like that of the National Assembly of France, sufficiently shows that the strength of government does not consist in any thing *within* itself, but in the attachment of a nation, and the interest which the people feel in supporting it. When this is lost, government is but a child in power; and though, like the old government of France, it may harass individuals for a while, it but facilitates its own fall.

After the Declaration of Independence, it became consistent with the principle on which representative government is founded, that the authority of Congress should be defined and established. Whether that authority should be more or less than Congress then discretionally exercised, was not the question. It was merely the rectitude of the measure.

For this purpose, the act, called the Act of Confederation (which was a sort of imperfect federal constitution), was proposed, and, after long deliberation, was concluded in the year 1781. It was not the act of Congress, because it is repugnant to the principles of representative government that a body should give power to itself. Congress first informed the several states of the powers which it conceived were necessary to be invested in the union, to enable it to perform the duties and services required from it; and the states severally agreed with each other, and concentrated in Congress those powers.

It may not be improper to observe, that in both those instances (the one of Pennsylvania, and the other of the United States), there is no such thing as the idea of a compact between the people on one side, and the government on the other. The compact was that of the people with each other, to produce and constitute a government.

To suppose that any government can be a party in a compact with the whole people, is to suppose it to have existence before it can have a right to exist. The only instance in which a compact can take place between the people and those who exercise the government, is, that the people shall pay them, while they choose to employ them.

Government is not a trade which any man or body of men has a right to set up and exercise for his own emolument, but is altogether a trust, in right of those by whom that trust is delegated, and by whom it is always resumable. It has of itself no rights; they are altogether duties.

Having thus given two instances of the original formation of a constitution, I will show the manner in which both have been changed since their first establishment.

The powers vested in the governments of the several States, by the State constitutions, were found, upon experience, to be too great; and those vested in the Federal Government, by the Act of Confederation, too little. The defect was not in the principle, but in the distribution of power.

Numerous publications, in pamphlets and in the newspapers, appeared on the propriety and necessity of new modelling the Federal Government. After some time of public discussion, carried on through the channel of the press, and in conversations, the State of Virginia, experiencing some inconvenience with respect to commerce, proposed holding a continental conference ; in consequence of which, a deputation from five or six of the State assemblies met at Annapolis in Maryland in 1786.

This meeting, not conceiving itself sufficiently authorized to go into the business of a reform, did no more than state their general opinions of the propriety of the measure, and recommended that a convention of all the States should be held the year following.

This convention met at Philadelphia in May 1787, of which General Washington was elected President. He was not at that time connected with any of the State governments, or with Congress. He delivered up his commission when the war ended, and since then had lived a private citizen. The convention went deeply into all the subjects ; and having, after a variety of debate and investigation, agreed among themselves upon the several parts of a Federal Constitution, the next question was, the manner of giving it authority and practise.

For this purpose, they did not, like a cabal of courtiers, send for a Dutch stadtholder, or a German elector ; but they referred the whole matter to the sense and interest of the country.

They first directed that the proposed Constitution should be published. Secondly, that each State should elect a convention, expressly for the purpose of taking it into consideration, and of ratifying or rejecting it ; and that as soon as the approbation and ratification of any nine States should be given, that those States should proceed to the election of their proportion of members to the new Federal Government ; and that the operation of it should then begin, and the former Federal Government cease.

The several States proceeded accordingly to elect their conventions. Some of those conventions ratified the Constitution by very large majorities, and two or three unanimously. In others there were much debate and division of opinion. In the Massachusetts Convention, which met at Boston, the majority was not above nineteen or twenty, in about three hundred members ; but such is the nature of representative government, that it quietly decides all matters by majority.

After the debate in the Massachusetts Convention was closed, and the vote taken, the objecting members rose, and declared, *"That though they had argued and voted against it, because certain parts appeared to them in a different light to what they appeared to other members : yet, as the vote had decided in favor of the Constitution as proposed, they should give it the same practical support as if they had voted for it."*

Government is but now beginning to be known. Hitherto it has been the mere exercise of power, which forbade all effectual inquiry into rights, and grounded itself wholly on possession. While the enemy of liberty was its judge, the progress of its principles must have been small indeed.

The constitutions of America, and also that of France, have either fixed a period for their revision, or laid down the mode by which improvements shall be made.

It is perhaps impossible to establish any thing that combines principles with opinions and practise, which the progress of circumstances, through a length of years, will not in some measure derange, or render inconsistent ; and therefore, to prevent inconveniences

accumulating, till they discourage reformations or provoke revolutions, it is best to regulate them as they
occur.

The rights of man are the rights of all generations of
men, and cannot be monopolized by any. That which
is worth following, will be followed for the sake of its
worth ; and it is in this that its security lies, and not in
any conditions with which it may be incumbered.
When a man leaves property to his heirs, he does not
connect it with an obligation that they shall accept it.
Why then should we do otherwise with respect to constitutions ?

The best constitution that could now be devised,
consistent with the condition of the present moment,
may be far short of that excellence which a few years
may afford. There is a morning of reason rising upon
man, on the subject of government, that has not appeared before. As the barbarism of the present old
governments expires, the moral condition of the nations, with respect to each other, will be changed.

Man will not be brought up with the savage idea of
considering his species as enemies, because the accident
of birth gave the individuals existence in countries distinguished by different names ; and as constitutions have
always some relation to external as well as domestic circumstances, the means of benefitting by every change,
foreign or domestic, should be a part of every constitution.

Government ought to be as much open to improvement as anything which appertains to man, instead of
which it has been monopolized from age to age, by the
most ignorant and vicious of the human race.   Need we
any other proof of their wretched management, than
the excess of debt and taxes with which every nation
groans, and the quarrels into which they have precipi-
tated the world ?

Just emerging from such a barbarous condition, it is

too soon to determine to what extent of improvement government may yet be carried. For what we can foresee, all Europe may form but one great republic, and man be free of the whole.

AGRARIAN JUSTICE

(1797)

To the Legislature and the Executive Directory of the French Republic

The plan contained in this work is not adapted for any particular country alone : the principle on which it is based is general. But as the rights of man are a new study in this world, and one needing protection from priestly imposture, and the insolence of oppressions too long established, I have thought it right to place this little work under your safeguard.

When we reflect on the long and dense night in which France and all Europe have remained plunged by their governments and their priests, we must feel less surprise than grief at the bewilderment caused by the first burst of light that dispels the darkness. The eye accustomed to darkness can hardly bear at first the broad daylight. It is by usage the eye learns to see, and it is the same in passing from any situation to its opposite.

As we have not at one instant renounced all our errors, we cannot at one stroke acquire knowledge of all our rights. France has had the honor of adding to the word *Liberty* that of *Equality* ; and this word signifies essentially a principle that admits of no gradation in the things to which it applies. But equality is often misunderstood, often misapplied, and often violated.

Liberty and *Property* are words expressing all those of our possessions which are not of an intellectual nature. There are two kinds of property. Firstly, natural property, or that which comes to us from the Creator of the universe — such as the earth, air, water.

Secondly, artificial or acquired property — the invention of men.

In the latter, equality is impossible ; for to distribute it equally it would be necessary that all should have contributed in the same proportion, which can never be the case ; and this being the case, every individual would hold on to his own property, as his right share. Equality of natural property is the subject of this little essay. Every individual in the world is born therein with legitimate claims on a certain kind of property, or its equivalent.

The right of voting for persons charged with the execution of the laws that govern society is inherent in the word liberty, and constitutes the equality of personal rights. But even if that right (of voting) were inherent in property, which I deny, the right of suffrage would still belong to all equally, because, as I have said, all individuals have legitimate birthrights in a certain species of property.

I have always considered the present Constitution of the French Republic the *best organized system* the human mind has yet produced. But I hope my former colleagues will not be offended if I warn them of an error which has slipped into its principle. Equality of the right of suffrage is not maintained. This right is in it connected with a condition on which it ought not to depend ; that is, with a proportion of a certain tax called "direct."

The dignity of suffrage is thus lowered ; and, in placing it in the scale with an inferior thing, the enthusiasm that right is capable of inspiring is diminished. It is impossible to find any equivalent counterpoise for the right of suffrage, because it is alone worthy to be its own basis, and cannot thrive as a graft, or an appendage.

Since the Constitution was established we have seen two conspiracies stranded — that of Babeuf, and that of some obscure personages who decorate themselves with the despicable name of "royalists." The defect in principle of the Constitution was the origin of Babeuf's conspiracy.

He availed himself of the resentment caused by this flaw, and instead of seeking a remedy by legitimate and constitutional means, or proposing some measure useful to society, the conspirators did their best to renew disorder and confusion, and constituted themselves personally into a Directory, which is formally destructive of election and representation. They were, in fine, extravagant enough to suppose that society, occupied with its domestic affairs, would blindly yield to them a directorship usurped by violence.

The conspiracy of Babeuf was followed in a few months by that of the royalists, who foolishly flattered themselves with the notion of doing great things by feeble or foul means. They counted on all the discontented, from whatever cause, and tried to rouse, in their turn, the class of people who had been following the others. But these new chiefs acted as if they thought society had nothing more at heart than to maintain courtiers, pensioners, and all their train, under the contemptible title of royalty. My little essay will disabuse them, by showing that society is aiming at a very different end — maintaining itself.

We all know or should know, that the time during which a revolution is proceeding is not the time when its resulting advantages can be enjoyed. But had Babeuf and his accomplices taken into consideration the condition of France under this Constitution, and compared it with what it was under the tragical revolutionary government, and during the execrable Reign of Terror, the rapidity of the alteration must have appeared to them very striking and astonishing. Famine has been replaced by abundance, and by the well-founded hope of a near and increasing prosperity.

As for the defect in the Constitution, I am fully convinced that it will be rectified constitutionally, and that this step is indispensable ; for so long as it continues it will inspire the hopes and furnish the means of conspirators ; and for the rest, it is regrettable that a Constitution so wisely organized should err so much in its principle. This fault exposes it to other dangers which will make themselves felt.

Intriguing candidates will go about among those who have not the means to pay the direct tax and pay it for them, on condition of receiving their votes. Let us maintain inviolably equality in the sacred right of suffrage : public security can never have a basis more solid. *Salut et Fraternité.*

Your former colleague,
THOMAS PAINE

Whether that state that is proudly, perhaps erroneously, called civilization, has most promoted or most injured the general happiness of man, is a question that may be strongly contested. On one side, the spectator is dazzled by splendid appearances ; on the other, he is shocked by extremes of wretchedness ; both of which it has erected. The most affluent and the most miserable of the human race are to be found in the countries that are called civilized.

To understand what the state of society ought to be, it is necessary to have some idea of the natural and primitive state of man ; such as it is at this day among the Indians of North America. There is not, in that state, any of those spectacles of human misery which poverty and want present to our eyes in all the towns and streets in Europe.

The life of an Indian is a continual holiday, compared with the poor of Europe ; and, on the other hand it appears to be abject when compared to the rich. Civilization, therefore, or that which is so called, has operated two ways : to make one part of society more affluent, and the other more wretched, than would have been the lot of either in a natural state.

It is always possible to go from the natural to the civilized state, but it is never possible to go from the civilized to the natural state. The reason is that man in a natural state, subsisting by hunting, requires ten times the quantity of land to range over to procure himself sustenance, than would support him in a civilized state, where the earth is cultivated.

When, therefore, a country becomes populous by the additional aids of cultivation, art and science, there is a necessity of preserving things in that state ; because without it there cannot be sustenance for more, perhaps, than a tenth part of its inhabitants. The thing, therefore, now to be done is to remedy the evils and preserve the benefits that have arisen to society by passing from the natural to that which is called the civilized state.

In taking the matter upon this ground, the first principle of civilization ought to have been, and ought still to be, that the condition of every person born into the world, after a state of civilization commences, ought not to be worse than if he had been born before that period.

But the fact is that the condition of millions, in every country in Europe, is far worse than if they had been born before civilization began, or had been born among the Indians of North America at the present day. I will show how this fact has happened.

It is a position not to be controverted that the earth, in its natural, uncultivated state was, and ever would have continued to be, *the common property of the human race*. In that state every man would have been born to property. He would have been a joint life proprietor with the rest in the property of the soil, and in all its natural productions, vegetable and animal.

But the earth in its natural state, as before said, is

capable of supporting but a small number of inhabitants compared with what it is capable of doing in a cultivated state. And as it is impossible to separate the improvement made by cultivation from the earth itself, upon which that improvement is made, the idea of landed property arose from that inseparable connection ; but it is nevertheless true, that it is the value of the improvement, only, and not the earth itself, that is individual property.

Every proprietor, therefore, of cultivated lands, owes to the community a *ground-rent* (for I know of no better term to express the idea) for the land which he holds ; and it is from this ground-rent that the fund proposed in this plan is to issue.

It is deducible, as well from the nature of the thing as from all the histories transmitted to us, that the idea of landed property commenced with cultivation, and that there was no such thing as landed property before that time. It could not exist in the first state of man, that of hunters. It did not exist in the second state, that of shepherds : neither Abraham, Isaac, Jacob, nor Job, so far as the history of the Bible may be credited in probable things, were owners of land.

Their property consisted, as is always enumerated in flocks and herds, and they traveled with them from place to place. The frequent contentions at that time about the use of a well in the dry country of Arabia, where those people lived, also show that there was no landed property. It was not admitted that land could be claimed as property.

There could be no such thing as landed property originally. Man did not make the earth, and, though he had a natural right to *occupy* it, he had no right to *locate as his property* in perpetuity any part of it ; neither did the Creator of the earth open a land-office, from whence the first title-deeds should issue. Whence then, arose the idea of landed property ? I answer as before, that when cultivation began the idea of landed property began with it, from the impossibility of separating the improvement made by cultivation from the earth itself, upon which that improvement was made.

The value of the improvement so far exceeded the value of the natural earth, at that time, as to absorb it ; till, in the end, the common right of all became confounded into the cultivated right of the individual. But there are, nevertheless, distinct species of rights, and will continue to be, so long as the earth endures.

It is only by tracing things to their origin that we can gain rightful ideas of them, and it is by gaining such ideas that we discover the boundary that divides right from wrong, and teaches every man to know his own. I have entitled this tract "Agrarian Justice" to distinguish it from "Agrarian Law."

Nothing could be more unjust than agrarian law in a country improved by cultivation ; for though every man, as an inhabitant of the earth, is a joint proprietor of it in its natural state, it does not follow that he is a joint proprietor of cultivated earth. The additional value made by cultivation, after the system was admitted, became the property of those who did it, or who inherited it from them, or who purchased it. It had originally no owner. While, therefore, I advocate the right, and interest myself in the hard case of all those who have been thrown out of their natural inheritance by the introduction of the system of landed property, I equally defend the right of the possessor to the part which is his.

Cultivation is at least one of the greatest natural improvements ever made by human invention. It has given to created earth a tenfold value. But the landed monopoly that began with it has produced the greatest evil. It has dispossessed more than half the inhabitants of every nation of their natural inheritance, without providing for them, as ought to have been done, an indemnification for that loss, and has thereby created a species of poverty and wretchedness that did not exist before.

In advocating the case of the persons thus dispossessed, it is a right, and not a charity, that I am pleading for.   But it is that kind of right which, being neglected at first, could not be brought forward afterwards till heaven had opened the way by a revolution in the system of government.   Let us then do honor to revolutions by justice, and give currency to their principles by blessings.

Having thus in a few words, opened the merits of the case, I shall now proceed to the plan I have to propose, which is,

To create a national fund, out of which there shall be paid to every person, when arrived at the age of twenty-one years, the sum of fifteen pounds sterling, as a compensation in part, for the loss of his or her natural inheritance, by the introduction of the system of landed property :

And also, the sum of ten pounds per annum, during life, to every person now living, of the age of fifty years, and to all others as they shall arrive at that age.

I have already established the principle, namely, that the earth, in its natural uncultivated state was, and ever would have continued to be, the *common property of the human race* ; that in that state, every person would have been born to property ; and that the system of landed property, by its inseparable connection with cultivation, and with what is called civilized life, has absorbed the property of all those whom it dispossessed, without providing, as ought to have been done, an indemnification for that loss.

The fault, however, is not in the present possessors. No complaint is intended, or ought to be alleged against them, unless they adopt the crime by opposing justice.

The fault is in the system, and it has stolen imperceptibly upon the world, aided afterwards by the agrarian law of the sword.   But the fault can be made to reform itself by successive generations ; and without diminishing or deranging the property of any of the present possessors, the operation of the fund can yet commence, and be in full activity, the first year of its establishment, or soon after, as I shall show.

It is proposed that the payments, as already stated, be made to every person, rich or poor.   It is best to make it so, to prevent invidious distinctions.   It is also right it should be so, because it is in lieu of the natural inheritance, which, as a right, belongs to every man, over and above the property he may have created, or inherited from those who did.   Such persons as do not choose to receive it can throw it into the common fund.

Taking it then for granted that no person ought to be in a worse condition when born under what is called a state of civilization, than he would have been had he been born in a state of nature, and that civilization ought to have made, and ought still to make, provision for that purpose, it can only be done by subtracting from property a portion equal in value to the natural inheritance it has absorbed.

Various methods may be proposed for this purpose, but that which appears to be the best (not only because it will operate without deranging any present possessors, or without interfering with the collection of taxes or *emprunts* necessary for the purposes of government and the Revolution, but because it will be the least troublesome and the most effectual, and also because the subtraction will be made at a time that best admits it) is at the moment that property is passing by the death of one person to the possession of another. In this case, the bequeather gives nothing : the receiver pays nothing.   The only matter to him is that the monopoly of natural inheritance, to which there never was a right, begins to cease in his person. A generous man would not wish it to continue, and a just man will rejoice to see it abolished.

Separate an individual from society, and give him an island or a continent to possess, and he cannot acquire personal property. He cannot be rich. So inseparably are the means connected with the end, in all cases, that where the former do not exist the latter cannot be obtained. All accumulation, therefore, of personal property, beyond what a man's own hands produce, is derived to him by living in society ; and he owes on every principle of justice, of gratitude, and of civilization, a part of that accumulation back again to society from whence the whole came.

This is putting the matter on a general principle, and perhaps it is best to do so ; for if we examine the case minutely it will be found that the accumulation of personal property is, in many instances, the effect of paying too little for the labor that produced it ; the consequence of which is that the working hand perishes in old age, and the employer abounds in affluence.

It is, perhaps, impossible to proportion exactly the price of labor to the profits it produces ; and it will also be said, as an apology for the injustice, that were a workman to receive an increase of wages daily he would not save it against old age, nor be much better for it in the interim. Make, then, society the treasurer to guard it for him in a common fund ; for it is no reason that, because he might not make a good use of it for himself, another should take it.

The state of civilization that has prevailed throughout Europe, is as unjust in its principle, as it is horrid in its effects ; and it is the consciousness of this, and the apprehension that such a state cannot continue when once investigation begins in any country, that makes the possessors of property dread every idea of a revolution. It is the hazard and not the principle of revolu tions that retards their progress. This being the case, it is necessary as well for the protection of property as for the sake of justice and humanity, to form a system that, while it preserves one part of society from wretchedness, shall secure the other from depredation.

The superstitious awe, the enslaving reverence, that formerly surrounded affluence, is passing away in all countries, and leaving the possessor of property to the convulsion of accidents. When wealth and splendor, instead of fascinating the multitude, excite emotions of disgust ; when, instead of drawing forth admiration, it is beheld as an insult upon wretchedness ; when the ostentatious appearance it makes serves to call the right of it in question, the case of property becomes critical, and it is only in a system of justice that the possessor can contemplate security.

To remove the danger, it is necessary to remove the antipathies, and this can only be done by making property productive of a national blessing, extending to every individual. When the riches of one man above another shall increase the national fund in the same proportion ; when it shall be seen that the prosperity of that fund depends on the prosperity of individuals ; when the more riches a man acquires, the better it shall be for the general mass ; it is then that antipathies will cease, and property be placed on the permanent basis of national interest and protection.

I have no property in France to become subject to the plan I propose. What I have, which is not much, is in the United States of America. But I will pay one hundred pounds sterling toward this fund in France, the instant it shall be established ; and I will pay the same sum in England, whenever a similar establishment shall take place in that country.

A revolution in the state of civilization is the necessary companion of revolutions in the system of government. If a revolution in any country be from bad to good, or from good to bad, the state of what is called civilization in that country, must be made conformable thereto, to give that revolution effect.

Despotic government supports itself by abject civilization, in which debasement of the human mind, and wretchedness in the mass of the people, are the chief criterions. Such governments consider man merely as an animal ; that the exercise of intellectual faculty is not his privilege ; *that he has nothing to do with the laws but to obey them* ; and they politically depend more upon breaking the spirit of the people by poverty, than they fear enraging it by desperation.

It is a revolution in the state of civilization that will give perfection to the Revolution of France. Already the conviction that government by representation is the true system of government is spreading itself fast in the world. The reasonableness of it can be seen by all. The justness of it makes itself felt even by its opposers. But when a system of civilization, growing out of that system of government, shall be so organized that not a man or woman born in the Republic but shall inherit some means of beginning the world, and see before them the certainty of escaping the miseries that under other governments accompany old age, the Revolution of France will have an advocate and an ally in the heart of all nations.

An army of principles will penetrate where an army of soldiers cannot ; it will succeed where diplomatic management would fail : it is neither the Rhine, the Channel, nor the ocean that can arrest its progress : it will march on the horizon of the world, and it will conquer.

THOMAS PAINE TO THE CITIZENS
OF THE UNITED STATES *

AND PARTICULARLY TO THE LEADERS OF THE FEDERAL FACTION

After an absence of almost fifteen years, I am again returned to the country in whose dangers I bore my share, and to whose greatness I contributed my part.

When I sailed for Europe, in the spring of 1787, it was my intention to return to America the next year, and enjoy in retirement the esteem of my friends, and the repose I was entitled to. I had stood out the storm of one revolution, and had no wish to embark in another. But other scenes and other circumstances than those of contemplated ease were allotted to me.

The French Revolution was beginning to germinate when I arrived in France. The principles of it were good, they were copied from America, and the men who conducted it were honest. But the fury of faction soon extinguished the one and sent the other to the scaffold. Of those who began that Revolution, I am almost the only survivor, and that through a thousand dangers. I owe this not to the prayers of priests, nor to the piety of hypocrites, but to the continued protection of Providence.

But while I beheld with pleasure the dawn of liberty rising in Europe, I saw with regret the lustre of it fading in America. In less than two years from the time of my departure some distant symptoms painfully suggested the idea that the principles of the Revolution were expiring on the soil that produced them.

I now know from the information I obtain upon the spot, that the impressions that then distressed me, for I

* From letters published in *The National Intelligencer*, 1802–1803.

171

was proud of America, were but too well founded. She was turning her back on her own glory, and making hasty strides in the retrograde path of oblivion. But a spark from the altar of *Seventy-six*, unextinguished and unextinguishable through the long night of error, is again lighting up, in every part of the Union, the genuine name of rational liberty.

A faction, acting in disguise, was rising in America which had lost sight of first principles. They were beginning to contemplate government as a profitable monopoly, and the people as hereditary property. It is, therefore, no wonder that the "Rights of Man" was attacked by that faction, and its author continually abused. But let them go on ; give them rope enough and they will put an end to their own insignificance. There is too much common sense and independence in America to be long the dupe of any faction, foreign or domestic.

But, in the midst of the freedom we enjoy, the licentiousness of the papers called Federal (and I know not why they are called so, for they are in their principles anti-federal and despotic), is a dishonor to the character of the country, and an injury to its reputation and importance abroad. They represent the whole people of America as destitute of public principle and private manners.

There is in America, more than in any other country, a large body of people who attend quietly to their farms, or follow their several occupations ; who pay no regard to the clamors of anonymous scribblers, who think for themselves, and judge of government, not by the fury of newspaper writers, but by the prudent frugality of its measures, and the encouragement it gives to the improvement and prosperity of the country ; and who, acting on their own judgment, never come forward in an election but on some important occasion.

When this body moves, all the little barkings of scribbling and witless curs pass for nothing. To say to this independent description of men, "You must turn out such and such persons at the next election, for they have taken off a great many taxes, and lessened the expenses of government, they have dismissed my son, or my brother, or myself, from a lucrative office, in which there was nothing to do" — is to show the cloven foot of faction, and preach the language of ill-disguised mortification.

As the affairs of the country to which I am returned are of more importance to the world, and to me, than of that I have lately left (for it is through the New World the Old must be regenerated, if regenerated at all), I shall not take up the time of the reader with an account of scenes that have passed in France, many of which are painful to remember and horrid to relate, but come at once to the circumstances in which I find America on my arrival.

Fourteen years, and something more, have produced a change, at least among a part of the people, and I ask myself what it is ? I meet or hear of thousands of my former connections, who are men of the same principles and friendships as when I left them. But a nondescript race, and of equivocal generation, assuming the name of *Federalist* — a name that describes no character of principle good or bad, and may equally be applied to either — has since started up with the rapidity of a mushroom, and like a mushroom is withering on its rootless stalk.

In the history of parties and the names they assume, it often happens that they finish by the direct contrary principles with which they profess to begin, and thus has happened with Federalism.

During the time of the old Congress, and pr establishment of the Federal Governme tinental belt was too loosely buckled. The several States were united in name but not in fact, and that nominal union had neither centre nor circle. The laws of one State frequently interfered with, and sometimes opposed, those of another. Commerce between State and State was without protection, and confidence without a point to rest on. The condition the country was then in was aptly described by Pelatiah Webster, when he said, "*thirteen staves and ne'er a hoop will not make a barrel.*"

If, then, by *Federalist* is to be understood one who was for cementing the Union by a general government operating equally over all the States, in all matters that embraced the common interest, and to which the authority of the States severally was not adequate, for no one State can make laws to bind another; if, I say, by a *Federalist* is meant a person of this description (and this is the origin of the name), *I ought to stand first on the list of Federalists*, for the proposition for establishing a general government over the Union, came originally from me in 1783, in a written memorial to Chancellor Livingston, then Secretary for Foreign Affairs to Congress, Robert Morris, Minister of Finance, and his associate, Gouverneur Morris, all of whom are now living; and we had a dinner ~ conference at Robert Morris's on the subject

As m~ ~ were minors are grown up
t~ ~ of *Federalist* began, it has
~formation, to go back and
which is now no longer
is the more necessary to
~rd, in the open face of
first called themselves

~endence, no period
~s the excellence of
~ent, and its superi-

ority over every other, as the time we now live in. Had America been cursed with John Adams's *hereditary Monarchy*, or Alexander Hamilton's *Senate for life*, she must have sought, in the doubtful contest of civil war, what she now obtains by the expression of public will. An appeal to elections decides better than an appeal to the sword.

The Reign of Terror that raged in America during the latter end of the Washington Administration, and the whole of that of Adams, is enveloped in mystery to me. That there were men in the Government hostile to the representative system, was once their boast, though it is now their overthrow, and therefore the fact is established against them.

But that so large a mass of the people should become the dupes of those who were loading them with taxes in order to load them with chains, and deprive them of the right of election, can be ascribed only to that species of wildfire rage, lighted up by falsehood that not only acts without reflection, but is too impetuous to make any.

There is a general and striking difference between the genuine effects of truth itself, and the effects of falsehood believed to be truth. Truth is naturally benign ; but falsehood believed to be truth is always furious. The former delights in serenity, is mild and persuasive, and seeks not the auxiliary aid of invention. The latter sticks at nothing.

It has naturally no morals. Every lie is welcome that suits its purpose. It is the innate character of the thing to act in this manner, and the criterion by which it may be known, whether in politics or religion. When anything is attempted to be supported by lying it is presumptive evidence that the thing so supported is a lie also. The stock on which a lie can be grafted must be of the same species as the graft.

As to the licentiousness of the papers calling themselves *Federal*, it can hurt nobody but the party or the persons who support such papers. There is naturally a wholesome pride in the public mind that revolts at open vulgarity. It feels itself dishonored even by hearing it, as a chaste woman feels dishonor by hearing obscenity she cannot avoid. It can smile at wit, or be diverted with strokes of satirical humor, but it detests the *blackguard*.

The event of the late election shows this to be true ; for in proportion as those papers have become more and more vulgar and abusive, the elections have gone more and more against the party they support, or that supports them.

The Spanish proverb says, *"there never was a cover large enough to hide itself"* ; and the proverb applies to the case of those papers and the shattered remnant of the faction that supports them. The falsehoods they fabricate, and the abuse they circulate, is a cover to hide something from being seen, but it is not large enough to hide itself. It is as a tub thrown out to the whale to prevent its attacking and sinking the vessel. They want to draw the attention of the public from thinking about, or inquiring into, the measures of the late Administration, and the reason why so much public money was raised and expended ; and so far as a lie today, and a new one tomorrow, will answer this purpose, it answers theirs. It is nothing to them whether they be believed or not, for if the negative purpose be answered the main point is answered, to them.

He that picks your pocket always tries to make you look another way. "Look," says he, "at yon man t'other side the street — what a nose he has got ? — Lord, yonder is a chimney on fire ! — Do you see yon man going along in the salamander great coat ? That is the very man that stole one of Jupiter's satellites, and sold it to a countryman for a gold watch, and it set his breeches on fire !"

Now the man that has his hand in your pocket, does not care a farthing whether you believe what he says or not. All his aim is to prevent your looking at *him* ; and this is the case with the remnant of the Federal faction. The leaders of it have imposed upon the country, and they want to turn the attention of it from the subject.

In taking up any public matter, I have never made it a consideration, and never will, whether it be popular or unpopular ; but whether it be *right* or *wrong*. The right will always become the popular, if it has courage to show itself, and the shortest way is always a straight line.

And all the world knows, for it cannot help knowing, that to judge *rightly* and to write *clearly*, and that upon all sorts of subjects, to be able to command thought and as it were to play with it at pleasure, and be always master of one's temper in writing, is the faculty only of a serene mind, and the attribute of a happy and philosophical temperament.

It is always the interest of a far greater part of the nation to have a thing right than to have it wrong ; and therefore, in a country whose government is founded on the system of election and representation, the fate of every party is decided by its principles.

Though hypocrisy can counterfeit every virtue, and become the associate of every vice, it requires a great dexterity of craft to give it the power of deceiving. A painted sun may glisten, but it cannot warm. For hypocrisy to personate virtue successfully it must know and feel what virtue is, and as it cannot long do this it cannot long deceive. When an orator foaming for war breathes forth in another sentence a *plaintive piety of words*, he may as well write HYPOCRISY on his front.

But hypocrisy is a vice of sanguine constitution. It

flatters and promises itself everything ; and it has yet to learn, with respect to moral and political reputation, it is less dangerous to offend than to deceive.

To the measures of Administration, supported by the firmness and integrity of the majority in Congress, the United States owe, as far as human means are concerned, the preservation of peace, and of national honor. The confidence which the Western people reposed in the Government and their representatives is rewarded with success. They are reinstated in their rights with the least possible loss of time ; and their harmony with the people of New Orleans, so necessary to the prosperity of the United States, which would have been broken, and the seeds of discord sown in its place, had hostilities been preferred to accommodation, remains unimpaired. Have the Federal ministers of the Church meditated on these matters ? and laying aside, as they ought to do, their electioneering and vindictive prayers and sermons, returned thanks that peace is preserved, and commerce, without the stain of blood ?

In the pleasing contemplation of this state of things the mind, by comparison, carries itself back to those days of uproar and extravagance that marked the career of the former Administration, and decides, by the unstudied impulse of its own feelings, that something must then have been wrong. Why was it that America, formed for happiness, and remote by situation and circumstances from the troubles and tumults of the European world, became plunged into its vortex and contaminated with its crimes ?

The answer is easy. Those who were then at the head of affairs were apostates from the principles of the Revolution. Raised to an elevation they had not a right to expect, nor judgment to conduct, they became like feathers in the air, and blown about by every puff of passion or conceit.

Candor would find some apology for their conduct

if want of judgment was their only defect. But error and crime, though often alike in their features, are distant in their characters and in their origin. The one has its source in the weakness of the head, the other in the hardness of the heart, and the coalition of the two describes the former Administration.

Had no injurious consequences arisen from the conduct of that Administration, it might have passed for error or imbecility, and been permitted to die and be forgotten. The grave is kind to innocent offense. But even innocence, when it is a cause of injury, ought to undergo an inquiry.

The country, during the time of the former Administration, was kept in continual agitation and alarm ; and that no investigation might be made into its conduct, it intrenched itself within a magic circle of terror, and called it a SEDITION LAW. Violent and mysterious in its measures and arrogant in its manners, it affected to disdain information, and insulted the principles that raised it from obscurity.

John Adams and Timothy Pickering were men whom nothing but the accidents of the times rendered visible on the political horizon. Elevation turned their heads, and public indignation has cast them to the ground. But an inquiry into the conduct and measures of that Administration is nevertheless necessary.

The country was put to great expense. Loans, taxes and standing armies became the standing order of the day. The militia, said Secretary Pickering, are not to be depended upon, and fifty thousand men must be raised. For what ? No cause to justify such measures has yet appeared. No discovery of such a cause has yet been made. The pretended Sedition Law shut up the sources of investigation, and the precipitate flight of John Adams closed the scene. But the matter ought not to sleep here.

It is not to gratify resentment, or encourage it in

others, that I enter upon this subject. It is not in the power of man to accuse me of a persecuting spirit. But some explanation ought to be had. The motives and objects respecting the extraordinary and expensive measures of the former Administration ought to be known. The Sedition Law, that shield of the moment, prevented it then, and justice demands it now.

If the public have been imposed upon, it is proper they should know it ; for where judgment is to act, or a choice is to be made, knowledge is first necessary. The conciliation of parties, if it does not grow out of explanation, partakes of the character of collusion or indifference.

There has been guilt somewhere ; and it is better to fix it where it belongs, and separate the deceiver from the deceived, than that suspicion, the bane of society, should range at large, and sour the public mind. The military measures that were proposed and carried on during the former Administration could not have for their object the defense of the country against invasion. This is a case that decides itself ; for it is self-evident, that while the war raged in Europe, neither France nor England could spare a man to send to America.

The object, therefore, must be something at home, and that something was the overthrow of the representative system of government, for it could be nothing else.

But ought a people who, but a few years ago, were fighting the battles of the world — for liberty had no home but here — ought such a people to stand quietly by and see that liberty undermined by apostasy and overthrown by intrigue ? Let the tombs of the slain recall their recollection, and the forethought of what their children are to be revive and fix in their hearts the love of liberty.

The suspicion against the late Administration is that

it was plotting to overturn the representative system of government, and that it spread alarms of invasions that had no foundation as a pretense for raising and establishing a military force as the means of accomplishing that object.

The law, called the Sedition Law, enacted, that if any person should write or publish, or cause to be written or published, any libel [without defining what a libel is] against the Government of the United States, or either House of Congress, or against the President, he should be punished by a fine not exceeding two thousand dollars, and by imprisonment not exceeding two years.

But it is a much greater crime for a President to plot against a constitution and the liberties of the people, than for an individual to plot against a President ; and consequently, John Adams is accountable to the public for his conduct, as the individuals under his Administration were to the Sedition Law.

THE WILL OF THOMAS PAINE

(January 1809)

The last Will and Testament of me, the subscriber, Thomas Paine, reposing confidence in my Creator, God, and in no other being, for I know of no other, nor believe in any other. I, Thomas Paine, of the State of New York, author of the work entitled "Common Sense," written in Philadelphia, in 1775, and published in that city the beginning of January 1776, which awaked America to a declaration of independence on the fourth of July following, which was as fast as the work could spread through such an extensive country ; author also of the several numbers of the "American Crisis," thirteen in all ; published occasionally during the progress of the Revolutionary War — the last is on the peace ; author also of "Rights of Man," parts the first and second, written and published in London, in 1791 and 1792 ; author also of a work on religion, "Age of Reason," parts the first and second — N. B. I have a third part by me in manuscript, and an answer to the Bishop of Llandaff ; author also of a work, lately published, entitled "Examination of the Passages in the New Testament, Quoted from the Old, and called Prophecies concerning Jesus Christ, and showing there are no Prophecies of any such Person" ; author also of several other works not here enumerated, "Dissertations on First Principles of Government — Decline and Fall of the English System of Finance — Agrarian Justice," etc., etc., make this my last will and testament, that is to say :

I give and bequeath to my executors hereinafter appointed, Walter Morton and Thomas Addis Emmet, thirty shares I hold in the New York Phœnix Insurance

Company, which cost me fourteen hundred and seventy dollars, they are worth now upwards of fifteen hundred dollars, and all my movable effects, and also the money that may be in my trunk or elsewhere at the time of my decease, paying thereout the expenses of my funeral, IN TRUST as to the said shares, movables, and money, for Margaret Brazier Bonneville, wife of Nicholas Bonneville, of Paris, for her own sole and separate use, and at her own disposal, notwithstanding her coverture.

As to my farm in New Rochelle, I give, devise, and bequeath the same to my said executors, Walter Morton and Thomas Addis Emmet, and to the survivor of them, his heirs and assigns for ever, IN TRUST nevertheless, to sell and dispose of the north side thereof, now in the occupation of Andrew A. Dean, beginning at the west end of the orchard, and running in a line with the land sold to —— Coles, to the end of the farm, and to apply the money arising from such sale as hereinafter directed.

I know not if the Society of people called Quakers, admit a person to be buried in their burying ground, who does not belong to their Society, but if they do, or will admit me, I would prefer being buried there ; my father belonged to that profession, and I was partly brought up in it. But if it is not consistent with their rules to do this, I desire to be buried on my own farm at New Rochelle.

The place where I am to be buried, to be a square of twelve feet, to be enclosed with rows of trees, and a stone or post and rail fence, with a headstone with my name and age engraved upon it, author of "Common Sense." I nominate, constitute, and appoint Walter Morton, of the New York Phœnix Insurance Company, and Thomas Addis Emmet, counselor at law, late of Ireland, and Margaret B. Bonneville, executors and executrix to this my last will and testament, requesting the said Walter Morton and Thomas Addis Emmet, that they will give what assistance they conveniently can to Mrs. Bonneville, and see that the children be well brought up. Thus placing confidence in their friendship, I herewith take my final leave of them and of the world.

I have lived an honest and useful life to mankind; my time has been spent in doing good, and I die in perfect composure and resignation to the will of my Creator, God. Dated the eighteenth day of January, in the year one thousand eight hundred and nine; and I have also signed my name to the other sheet of this will, in testimony of its being a part thereof.

THOMAS PAINE